THOMAS
PAINE
PRESS

BOOKS BY VERNE FAUST

I Know More About you Than you Ever Dreamed Possible

VERNE FAUST

THOMAS PAINE PRESS
San Diego, California

PERMISSIONS

The author wishes to thank the following sources for permission to quote material for this book:

Roderic Gorney, M.D., for material from *The Human Agenda*, published by the Guild Tutors Press, 1019 Gayley Avenue, Los Angeles, California 90024. Copyright— 1972.

Dr. Harold Greenwald for material from *Direct Decision Therapy*. San Diego: EDITS, Publisher. Copyright— 1973.

Little, Brown and Company, Boston, for material from *Griefs and Discontents: The Forces of Change,* by Gregory Rochlin, M.D. Copyright—1965.

Phi Delta Kappa Foundation; Bloomington, Indiana, for material from *Values In Education,* by Max Lerner, Copyright— 1976.

For material: From "How People Change" by Allen Wheelis, *Commentary,* May 1969, by permission; copyright©1969 by the American Jewish Committee.

ACKNOWLEDGMENTS

While many individuals close to me have contributed to what has been shared on these pages, several have read the manuscript during its development and offered encouragement, recommending additions, deletions and other alterations.

Among these were Dr. Suzanne Faust, private practice psychologist, Las Vegas, Nevada; Dr. Roderic Gorney, psychiatrist-psychoanalyst, University of California Department of Psychiatry, and author of *The Human Agenda*; Fran Thorn; Debra Peterson and Ted Pessin.

Priceless contributions were provided by Dr. John Zell, psychiatrist-psychoanalyst, Phoenix, Arizona, and Beverly Zell, who together not only supplied invaluable suggestions in the manuscript's development, but whose encouragement made it possible to use a down-to-earth style of communication that would most likely reach the wide, general readership for which it was intended.

Finally, thanks to Nancy Skolnik, President of Thomas Paine Press, whose interest, encouragement and assistance reached far beyond what authors might expect. Her professional judgments and suggestions proved to be indispensable.

DEDICATION

Suzanne Faust

Who provided a profoundly deep relationship without which I could hardly have freed my sensitivity to discoveries shared here. Her capacity for such a relationship, spontaneity for entering into it, risking and sharing her person are limitless. She touched, entered, the deepest regions of my person. Without her I could not have fully become, nor would it have been possible to arrive at this moment of sharing with you.

CONTENTS

CONTENTS

PART FOUR

DEALING WITH YOUR PRODUCT- CENTERED RELATIONSHIPS

CONTENTS

PART FIVE

TAKING RIGHT AND WRONG, GOOD AND BAD, OUT OF SEX

CONTENTS

PART SIX

CONTENTS

PREFACE

I know more about you than you ever dreamed possible. I know that a part of you painfully needs to be valued more than people usually value you. I know that deep inside, hidden from others, you resent having to give right answers, feel right feelings, think right thoughts, and behave in right ways in order to be loved!

In countless ways, disguised from yourself and others, you search for a deep relationship with someone who values you, gives affection, touches and loves you because of your total impact, including the positives and the negatives. You want to be loved whether or not you fit into someone's snug set of "rights" and "goods." You need to have ALL of who you are sized up and valued. When loved only partially, touched conditionally, a wall of resentment begins to separate you from the one you love.

"Take me as I am," you say, "the whole, complete, total, overall impact I have on you. Allow me to be a human being," you ask.

"Let me have my:

frailties,
strengths,
consistencies
inconsistencies,
puzzling fantasies and
sometimes dumb ways.

"Love me when I'm:

sometimes dull,
exciting,
disorganized,
too organized,
insipid,
alive,
happy,
sad,
dissatisfied,
gregarious,
solitary,
lonely,
funny,
behind the times,
too ahead of the times,
shy,
tender,
loving,
bold,
sexual,
touching,
clinging and
free. . .without having
to be right, not wrong;
good, not bad.

"Believe in me," you ask. "Believe in my membership among humankind."

How can I say that I know all this about you even though we've never met? To begin with, on the pages that follow I'll share the reports of 220 million Americans and 25 million Canadians — reports which mirror your own suffering or that of persons close to you. These reports cast shadows of you and loved ones who have become addicted to product-centered love, darkly forecasting painful relationships and unnecessary seiges of ill health.

I Have Been There and I Found You

Much of what you feel, I feel. From this I know you better. I've been there where you learned to be you: in families and schools and communities. I know the parents and teachers who taught you who you are. They also taught me.

I've been there, experiencing life under a canopy of middle-class schools, ghetto classrooms and neighborhoods, and affluent suburbs. My hours have been spent in juvenile detention homes, courts, jails, therapy rooms, universities and mental hospitals. I've been there and found you. And I found me.

This book challenges much of what we have been told since childhood about how to live our own lives. Though most of these "ways" thwart our happiness and health, we are inclined to stay with them, indeed do not question their "rightness." Tenaciously we cling to what is familiar, warding off the unfamiliar even when freedom from personal and physical misery might be the reward for changing.

So it is that I invite you on a journey which, all along the way, questions your most used, basic ways of getting people to love you. Only when looking beyond customary ways of seeing yourself and others can you experience dimensions of your life that you never dreamed possible.

VERNE FAUST

United States International University

San Diego, California

19

INTRODUCTION

BREAKING FREE OF OPPRESSIVE
"RIGHT" AND "GOOD,"
"WRONG" AND "BAD"

Efforts to control people with "right" and "good," "wrong" and "bad" aren't working. They never have. In fact, the results are a disaster.

In ridding ourselves of these methods, what do we use instead? What do we say and do, so that we can have a society which cares about itself and others? What methods can insure individuals, you and me, that a reasonable share of self esteem, love, and physical well-being can be enjoyed?

In place of time-worn, moralistic labels, this book suggests that you consider what I call *IMPACT-centered evaluations in your relationships with yourself and others.*

Along with examining new ways of what you can do, impact evaluations remove labels of right and wrong, good and bad from your thoughts, feelings and actions. Only when you view yourself and others free of these can you nurture and keep deep relationships, enjoy your share of happiness, and avoid unnecessary illnesses and a premature death.

Impact ways of living aren't the only answers. Life is complicated, of course, and an infinite number of pressures shape each individual's existence. Still, simple as it seems, seeing oneself and others in impact-centered ways, replacing moralistic labels, significant changes in a healthy direction can take place for you. Indeed, were an entire society—its families, communities, schools and governing bodies—to use impact evaluations, we could anticipate a remarkably different kind of world.

Does all this sound simplistic? Overstated? Does it smack of yet another panacea?

Not so.

I recognize the complex nature of happiness and unhappiness, physical health and ill health and death. People become happy or unhappy for a variety of reasons. They get along with one another or don't get along as a result of a myriad of conditions. Furthermore, in the case of sickness, germs do exist, people get sick and die whether or not they're happy. This is of course obvious.

My purpose is to focus on the key role that moralistic evaluations play as a major culprit in human misery. Resentment breeds in promises of love given for doing what is right and good; it flourishes out of the mire of withdrawn love for having been wrong and bad.

For some of you, in discovering impact centered ways of living, a whole new, exciting world will open up. Those of you, on the other hand, who choose to continue buying self esteem and love with moralistic currencies, will nevertheless do so out of a new awareness. Try as you may, whatever course you choose, you will never be the same again.

I write the book but the book writes me.

Johann Wolfgang von Goethe

How can human beings—'poor forked
radishes', all of us, with 'heads
fantastically carved' —learn and
grow in such a way that
our jumbled lives, our
mutilated psyches, our
dangerous endowment, our
stumbling blunder-beset
lives gain more meaning?

Max Lerner, 1976[120]

PART ONE

YOUR NEED
FOR A DEEP
RELATIONSHIP

YOU CAN'T BE PERFECT FOR OTHERS

However warm it feels to be rewarded with approval for doing what is right and good and wanted by others, somewhere deep inside, you resent this. At subtle levels you become apprehensive. "I must continue to live up to standards of other people. I must give them more of the products they require." You find that getting approval is a moment-to-moment affair, hinging on whether someone says that what you've thought, felt and done are right. Sooner or later you're judged "wrong" and they withdraw love.

At times you can't be the kind of wife, husband, daughter, son, lover or citizen that's required. You can't be the student others want you to be. You experience difficulties with mathematics, nor can you always write eloquent prose. Your hairstyle, political position, ideas on art, food, drink and clothing, all of these products may trigger dissatisfaction in people around you.

Like everyone, you're a limited human being. At times you're unpredictable, vulnerable to the vagaries of life, struggling to grow as a person. Being human in these ways, you can't afford to find self esteem and love by trying to say the right things or otherwise trying to be loved in payment for being good. There are, as I'll show, other more certain and satisfying ways to be valued.

Product-centered Love an Insatiable Appetite

When you try to be loved by giving people the kind of products they want, you live life in a constant, never fully satisfying effort to please. This puts you in a dangerous sort of human condition. No one can consistently produce products that always please others.

The actor whose name is suddenly in lights across the nation suffers a gnawing certainty that such acclaim is short-lived. More successes, greater and greater products are required to maintain a sense of personal worth. Academy Award winner Jack Lemmon said, "I didn't even like myself until I was past age thirty . . . . I thought I was supposed to measure up to some kind of image."[1]

The student whose paper is marked A-plus, with "Excellent!" scrawled across the top beams with temporary satisfaction. Soon more papers must be written to once again prove a sense of worth, however briefly.

Your Life as a Continuous Report Card

All your life you've been told, in one way or another, that you "can do it better." You found that the way you were was so unacceptable that they sent you off to school to change you. They wanted you to change from being a nonreader to someone who could read. All kinds of new products were demanded. "A's," "gold stars" and "happy faces" stamped on your products announced to you and the world that you were a good person. Every six weeks your "goodness" or "mediocrity" or "badness" were sent home on a report card. You learned to see yourself according to ways people evaluated your products, learned to "live up to" or "live down to" labels fastened on what you said and did.

Early Mother

Your bladder and bowels were full and without waiting you emptied them. Life was that simple, that easy. Infancy was mostly pleasure — *your* pleasure — whether filling your diaper, falling irresistably asleep, sucking from your mother's breast, or being enveloped in her arms, close to her warm body. You were touched by her, held, fed, bathed and cared for because you were you, without having to do things right or be a good person. Your summoning cries for help brought someone to remove the pain, rid you of stress, and restore a sense of safety. This someone usually turned out to be one person more than any other. We call this person "mother."

It wasn't that these goals — learning to read, write and do math — were unworthy. The destructiveness was in how they tried to get you to achieve these aims, in tying success to your worth as a person. This, as I'll show, breeds resentment in you, and eventually destroys your general happiness and physical health.

YOU HAD TWO MOTHERS

Those females or males who mothered you during your earliest weeks and months I'll call *Early Mother*. In most cultures this turns out to be a female, of course, so I'll refer to your Early Mother as "she" or "her."

Early Mother loved you for the total IMPACT that you had on her. Because you seemed totally helpless and not responsible for what you did, she loved and valued you whether you cried, smiled, drank milk or refused it, filled your diaper, slept or stayed awake when she thought you should be sleeping.

This is not to say that your Early Mother didn't get fatigued with you, exhausted, irritated, even exasperated. Still, you were not thought to be responsible for your behavior, not held accountable, and so were loved for total you — including all your frailties and penchant for doing things that worried her or did not make life easy.

Whatever your impact on Early Mother, you were not controlled by her with labels of right and good, wrong and bad. In order to win support and love no expectations were placed on you to behave in particular ways. You didn't have to change in any way as a condition of being valued. You could be you, total you, with the full range of your impact spent freely and safely on the world.

Where Your Need of a Deep Relationship Began

So it was that in the beginning all of your behavior was permissible. When your sphincter muscles gave the signal your bowels went into action and you relieved yourself. If the product turned out to be uncomfortable in your diaper you let it be known. A smiling face arrived and refreshed you with a clean diaper.

Soon you began to experience what it was like to be in touch with someone who seemed to care fully for you, who accepted whatever your behavior products might be. When in stress, wailing your dissatisfaction to the world, this person came to you. She touched you, interacted with you, and soon pleasure returned. You felt comfortable, safe.

Whatever your behavior during those earliest weeks — releasing your bowels and bladder, demanding to be fed, or insisting on being held, you were accepted and supported by her. Moreover, through it all she didn't convey that you were wrong or bad, nor in any way suggest that you had to be good and do things the right way in order to be loved.

It was during this period that your deepest, most permanent experiences would take place. Interacting with her in ways that were free of moralistic "rights and wrongs," "goods and bads," you experienced a sense of safety that bound you together. Your binding would color and change all your future relationships. It was here, with Early Mother, that you were imprinted with a need for a deep relationship.

When eventually it became apparent that Early Mother had been replaced by Later Mother, you began your life-long search for a new deep relationship. Your search would not be for Early Mother, of course, but for someone who could provide characteristics like those she shared with you. You had been imprinted forever with a need to be bonded to someone who could love you free of moralistic conditions placed upon your behavior.

A Binding That Frees You

One of your strongest drives is to be independent. You must have a sense of choosing the course of your behavior. At the same time, however, you never lose your need to be dependent on someone, like it was during those mostly pleasurable days with Early Mother.

You want to feel bound but at the some time free, a binding that feels unbound, a dependency that makes you feel independent. You search for someone who will love you for the total impact of who you are, including your frailties, strengths, assets and the full range of your thoughts and feelings. Whatever you think or feel or do, you want to know that you won't be rejected into a sea of guilt. You don't want to be manipulated with praise or criticism. It is your nature to want feedback of every conceivable kind regarding the kind of impact your behavior has had on others, but you require it to be free of moralistic evaluations. Only inside such a relationship can you hope to reach your goals for a satisfying life.[2]

Little wonder that your life-long yearning is for someone who :is:

Tender, gentle
Smiling,laughing,
Strong, supportive,
Touching, stimulating and
most important of all
*Capable of loving and accepting
the way you are.*

It was just such a person who was, in all likelihood, your Early Mother. These qualities, this kind of relationship, started you on your life-long search for intimacy and love with a person who could enter into a similar deep relationship, who would not try to control you with guilt, shame or anxiety about being right or wrong in what you do.

Wooden Puppet Love

In what we need most — a deep relationship such as I have described here — we are least successful in getting for ourselves. We yearn for it, search for it, yet time and again it eludes us.

Evidence of this is all around us. For example, out of every 10 marriages in urban areas there are nearly 8 divorces. Nationally the ratio is 10 to 5.[3] In product-centered relationships — based on getting love by being right or good—what was once warm, pulsating intimacy and profound feelings of affection, dry out and become wooden. Losing deep relationships has devastating effects. Suffering from disappointment and anger at being left, abandoned, millions flounder on shores of self-doubt and lonliness.

Out of this comes resentment. Too painful to bear, feeling guilty and afraid of the rage that resentment ultimately triggers, emotions of all kinds — especially anger — are buried in the unconscious self. A lid falls on all feelings, the person is left miserably depressed. "Depression," Dr. Rochlin[4] says, "is the psychology of disappointment." Some 15 of every 100 adults, twenty million Americans, at times suffer serious, excruciating depression.[5]

Your Greatest Disappointment

There's no greater disappointment than losing a deep relationship. Early in life you found that to avoid such a loss you were required to behave in expected ways. Do things "right," you found, qualifies you for praise, acclaim, adulation, self-respect and love. As long as you woodenly follow whatever course has been charted for you, the chances of losing self-worth lessen. Yet there's no way to win. Spending your days trying to do what is right and good, being worthy of daily handouts of self esteem, you soon grow resentful.

It is not only your nature to require a sense of self-worth and love, but equally so you need these without having to earn them with being "right" and "good" while avoiding "wrong" and "bad." When manipulated with moralistic promises and threats you feel like a puppet without control of your own personal safety and destiny. Placed in this precarious position, however much you succeed in being right and good, you resent your anxious state. Relationships based on moralisms soon splinter, either subtly hidden beneath the surface or openly splitting down the middle. Resentment is the ax that splinters more relationships than anything else.

Most who suffer the loss of a deep relationship soon begin their search anew, only vaguely aware of what it is that they hunger. They wish only, on the surface of awareness, to fill their emptiness. Unknown to themselves they seek someone who won't require them to be "right" and "good" as prerequisites to love. They search for someone who will respond to the overall impact of their self, with that response free of moralistic labels being tacked on. IMPACT centered relationships, replacing good-bad product-centered relationships is, knowingly or not, an effort to live once again inside the comfort, pleasure and reasonable security enjoyed with Early Mother.

LATER MOTHER

Your First Rejections

During your earliest weeks the binding to your mother didn't require you to do and think and say things right nor be a good person, but this soon changed. Early Mother faded away and was replaced by Later Mother. All-giving, non-controlling Early Mother abandoned you to becoming more grown up and on your own. YOU WERE LEFT!

Among other things, you were made to give up taking your meals from a nipple. Eventually you were expected to feed yourself—in just the right way. You couldn't play in your food and dump it over the side of the feeding chair, and when you got the mess all over your face you were promptly wiped clean. Things had to be "right" about you. When your behavior pleased those powerful people in your life, you dimly began to discover that they valued you more. Being right and good became an important part of being loved and safe as a person.

When Being "Right" Started to Mean Being "Good"

You began to sense that when you did things like Later Mother wanted, her demeanor took on certain characteristics. Her eyes, facial muscles and expressions changed. Her tone of voice, body postures, all signaled that you had performed in her expected ways. You discovered that there was something in the world called "being right." In fact her messages said that you were more than right. You were a *good person*.

Insidiously you became convinced that "right" was synonymous with "good." If you were to be a good person, first you had to think, feel and do things in the right ways. Most of all, if you were to be valued and loved, you found it necessary to be the sort of person that they call "good."

During your first months with Early Mother, when your bowels were full you merely eased their products into your diaper. While in the past a smiling face came to clean and refresh you, this changed. The smiles began to disappear. The products of your elimination took on a new meaning; people no longer accepted these products in your diaper. You sensed that you were not acceptable unless you produced:

the right product,

at the right place (in the toilet)

with the right texture (not too hard, not too soft)

the right color (not too dark)

the right amount (not holding any back)

and the right number of times per day.

At each elimination you may have been given a complete bowel report. Had you eliminated on time? Produced a sufficient quantity with correct texture? Was it too odorous?

Elimination Feelings

Those earliest efforts to control you linger on. You had to change. In order to gain her smiles and relaxed approval you had to produce products in her kind of way, in her kind of place.

At first you didn't catch on, didn't quite know what it was she wanted. You only knew that something was "wrong." She wasn't relaxed with you, as comfortable. It didn't feel as "good" with her sometimes.

Then you figured it out. Produce products her way, hold onto them for now and later deposit it all in a toilet. This somehow made it all right with her, between the two of you. Once again, having done it right, you were rewarded with comfortable feelings in your relationship. Soon you began to identify this with being good — a good person.

So it was that Later Mother gave you a different set of signals than Early Mother. Her eyes, voice and face conveyed rejection. It became clear that there was something about you that the world called "wrong." When you thought, felt or acted in wrong ways, messages were received that said you were more than wrong. You were a bad person. So that you might avoid this label you began to do what they wanted, and to do it right.

You had been trained. You learned to jump through one of the earliest hoops held up for you. When you produced as expected, they fed morsels of affection to you as rewards. On the other hand, when you missed, emptying your bowels in your pants, you were made to feel awful about yourself. Before long you began to identify with your own unacceptable products.

Time and again you saw your mother throw your products away, flushing them down the toilet. In later years, remnants of these earlier experiences would be translated into statements like:

"He treats me like I'm not worth shit."

Self-references would, more and more, get into the everyday language of living:

"I had a real shitty day at the office."
"He made me feel like a real shit."
"What a shitty feeling I got from him."

All kinds of expectations were made. For example, not only did you have to replace grunting and crying with speaking, but the words had to be pronounced right and spoken at the right times. Like bowel behavior, certain words were unclean, naughty, and you were wrong — bad — whenever you unloaded them in public. You soon learned that these were dirty words.

Only when your words, face and hands were clean, your toys, clothes and room picked up and neat, were you a good person. To do everything right was to be good.

Having to Be Good Made You Mad — Still Does

These conditions for being lovable eventually made you up-tight, literally. You started your life-long efforts to resist right and wrong labels. Not only did you avoid emptying your bowels in your pants, you didn't evacuate them at all. You held onto your products, held them up tight, refusing to part with any portion.

Your constipation upset Later Mother. Your resistance made her have to deal with you. For the moment, at least, you were in charge of the situation. A temporary surge of power was felt by you and, being in control, a personal sense of safety returned.

By age two or three your resistance went beyond bowel constipation. During the so-called negative period of the "terrible twos" you had the guts to say "no" to almost every request made of you.

"No," "I won't" and "I don't want to" were said a hundred times a day. Valiantly, while all the time upsetting others, you drove ruthlessly toward establishing your independence. Sometimes you were less direct, resisting in subtle ways. The older you grew, in fact, the more necessary it became to disguise efforts to free yourself.

You learned to veil resistance, hiding it from even yourself, relieving you of guilt. On the other hand, when you openly rebelled you got it in the end, sometimes with an enema. You were forced to produce expected products.

Toilet Relationships

Echoes of the past can be heard in: "I'm going to tell him to shove it up his ass!" This is to say that he's going to be forced, as in childhood, to produce expected behavior or suffer the consequences.

"A real shitty relationship" eventually developed between you and Later Mother. It was painful. You have managed to forget most of it, however, denying that it ever happened. To whatever extent you've repressed these memories and feelings, today they influence a major part of your relationships. In fact the more deeply buried the memories of Later Mother's attempts to control you with right and wrong, the less you are in charge of your life today.

GIVING UP CONSTIPATION
IN YOUR RELATIONSHIPS WITH PEOPLE

Spontaneity and Risking

You may still be holding back much of what you have to give in your relationships. Trying to be the kind of person that others want you to be ends in not being able to trust your own impulses. No longer can you give rein to your own feelings and ideas that are ready to burst into great, colorful, creative expressions.

Cautiously you guard feelings and ideas, careful to share only those that fit expectations of other people. Your more creative self is barred from the world, never reaching awareness. Your relationships have become constipated. Only in guarded ways, certain to insulate your self esteem, you share significant thoughts, feelings and touch. Superficial expressions, rather than deeper, more spontaneous reflections of who you are reach the people in your life.

Your Busy Censor

Before you speak or move or reach out in spontaneous, open ways, your censor checks to see if your products will be acceptable to other people. At that moment fresh spontaneity is lost. Your behavior has been distorted to fit what others expect. You've become like everyone else. You're now acceptable, almost.

Afraid to risk, letting your impulses, feelings and ideas flow without censor, you pay a price. The cost to personal happiness and, eventually, physical health is exhorbitant.

A High Price to Pay: Tunnel Vision

In a thousand unspoken ways you're directed to be who other people want you to be. In order to be loved you've put on blinders of a horse and narrowed your vision so that only a road already rutted by earlier travelers can be followed.

When you focus on teachers' answers, textbook writers' ideas, parents' values, spouse's expectations, and culture's biases, excluding your own lest you lose self esteem, walls begin to close around you.

It's written, or so it seems, on banners flown over your life that: Whatever you do, don't risk joyful spontaneity. Don't ad lib life but play it straight, as the lines were written for you. Methodically play life's countless scenes as they were penned by persons who have taken it upon themselves to be playwrights of your destiny.

Psychoanalyst John Zell[6] has said:

Essentially the survival approach has you living your life to please someone else. The child who complies, producing the 'right' products, pays a horrendous price. He becomes detached from his own impulses, surrenders spontaneity, putting aside ability to create and enjoy. He becomes the most impressive monument to the failure of our culture at this time.

FICTION OF RIGHT AND WRONG, GOOD AND BAD

Right and wrong, good and bad have no existence or reality of their own. They're merely human interpretations of things and events. These labels — and they're no more than that — vary from person to person, culture to culture, and time to time. At one point in history, for example, to wear a bathing suit that showed any portion of the body above the knee was wrong and labeled "bad." Today, of course, this interpretation has changed. Good and bad are obviously abstractions — they have no concrete existence of their own. They exist only in the minds of people, not the act itself.

As a human being you are an object. You have a body and body parts, such as heart and lungs. You are also a process, made up of circulating blood, digesting food, and experiences of thoughts and feelings. But you aren't a "good" or a "bad." You or other people simply label yourself as good or bad. If you accept these fictions about yourself as real, *really* see yourself as right or wrong, good or bad, you must pay a price for it, higher in personal and physical costs than you ever thought possible.

2 + 2 = 4 Is Not 'Right'

"But I know, for sure, that some things are 'right' and some are 'wrong,'" you say. "For example, two plus two equal four, and that's *right!* And two plus two equal three is *wrong*. It just is!"

I must answer that two plus two equal four is NOT right. Rather, it's *accurate*. It conforms to or fits an approved or conventional standard. It's "accurate" within a system arbitrarily devised or accepted by people as a prescribed way of doing something.

Consequently when you've added two dollars plus two dollars together on your luncheon check and get the sum of four dollars, which you pay to the cashier, you've not only accurately behaved according to a system agreed on by people in general, but your behavior has been *effective*. Adding two dollars and two dollars, and paying four dollars, WORKS. The cashier says, "Thank you," you both smile, and you walk out of the restaurant feeling, knowing, that the transaction has been effectively carried out. Your thinking and behaving worked for you and the cashier.

When you view your thoughts, feelings and actions in this way, doing so consistently in all matters, you begin to discover new attitudes about yourself. Throwing aside customary ways of seeing whatever you do as being right and good, wrong and bad, or some shade of these, and looking instead at your behavior with the questions WAS IT EFFECTIVE, DID IT WORK, old resentments toward yourself and others will melt. Guilt can dissolve, giving your spontaneous relationship with life a chance.

To Be 'Right' Is to Be Righteous, Good and Proper

The destructiveness in using the words "right" or "good" is in the deeper meaning that these have. On becoming aware of the destructive influence of these terms, we must think through what it is we are doing to very young children when using "right" and "good" as our chief way of teaching them. This holds true, also, for our schools. Teachers rely almost totally on getting students to learn by giving them rewarding words of "right" and "good " or some other symbol which means the same thing, such as a gold star fixed to a product, or a 'happy face' stamped on it, or an "A" letter grade.

These word messages serve as control methods throughout a lifetime, getting into your intimate relationships, friendships, and work. This way of reacting to yourself, grading your thoughts, feelings and actions on some right-wrong basis is, more than anything else, responsible for your resentment and self-depreciation.

Right-wrong product-centered ways of evaluating yourself and others are so much a part of everyone's life, is so rampant in society— the axle on which almost all human relationships turn — that they go unquestioned. It is easy to lose sight, indeed never become aware of what the deeper meaning these word evaluations have for your self esteem and body health.

While for many years being aware of what we *really* are saying about someone when evaluating what they've done as "right," I've been convinced that society has deeply buried the meaning of this word. However, in going to a dictionary for the generally accepted meaning of "right" it is obvious that, though covered surfacely, people do indeed at some unconscious levels understand that this word carries a heavy moralistic message. Clearly, as well, the dictionary emphasizes "right" to have more to do with being good and righteous, as in a religious way, than it does with accuracy or correctness.

PART TWO

YOU NEEDN'T GET SICK OR DIE BEFORE AGE 100

A few tranquil ones, with little conflict, suffer less; at the other extreme, stretched by despair to some dreadful cracking point, one goes beserk. In between are the rest of us, not miserable enough to go mad or jump off a bridge, yet never able, if we are honest, to say that we have come to terms with life, are at peace with ourselves, that we are happy.

Allen Wheelis[121]

THE 5% HYPOTHESIS

Most illnesses and deaths before age 100 are unnecessary. Said another way, based on my observation and interpretations of research, only 5% of sickness and dying needs to happen at all before finishing your first century of living. Furthermore, I'm convinced that when humankind learns how to behave with children and teenagers, life expectancy could reach more than 150 years.

You Don't Need to Have Unhappy, Sick Relationships

A majority of you are unable to keep a healthy, satisfying relationship with someone you love. In a small percentage who do manage to stay together, often the partners do so at exhorbitant costs to emotional and physical well-being. Human misery experienced by persons close to one another in love relationships is almost too painful to assemble inside the pages of a single book.

More effective ways, ones that work, are available to yourself and others. You don't have to live with periodic or chronic illnesses and die an early death. Nor must you continue destroying your intimate relationships or put up with less than a happy life. We human beings have evolved in ways that make it possible to live in relative happiness for at least a century.

HOW YOU SEE YOURSELF MAKES YOU WELL OR SICK

As an infant, before your sense of self emerged, nature took care of your body. Later, however, when you discovered that you were a person, this changed. Your self began to take charge of your body.

What you feel and think about yourself—your self-picture—can't be separated from how your body works. Your self and body work as one process; each affects the other.

It's true of course that germs sometimes attack bodies of people who for the most part are happy and successful. In other words happy persons DO get sick. Furthermore as years pass, time insidiously wears out organs; cells don't replenish in the same way as before. All people, happy and unhappy, get sick and eventually die. Yet with adequate dietary and other living conditions, in each person's 100 years more often than not it's apparent that disease and death might be traced to a negative self-picture and buried resentment. Science continues to be humankind's indispensable ally, medicine its benevolent support system. Both move forward together in warding off disease and preserving the body against death.

Yet the ravages of self-doubt, lonliness, guilt, resentment and buried rage toward our manipulators continue to make us vulnerable to disease and early death. Even with medicine's remarkable advances, it becomes your own choice whether to live happier, healthier and longer than you ever dreamed possible.

RESENTMENT DESTROYS YOUR RELATIONSHIPS, HAPPINESS, HEALTH AND LIFE

Where Most of Your Resentment Comes From

When safety is threatened, your body tries to protect itself by running away or attacking the source of danger. This is true whether the threat is to your body or self esteem. When endangered, you get inner signals that warn you to do something about it. Most common of these are anxiety, guilt, fear and body tension. You'll go to great lengths to rid yourself of them.

While lower animals either flee or attack the danger, humankind doesn't always have these options, at least so it seems. Many individuals, consequently, stay in a marriage or job though suffering painful anxiety.

Joining Those Who Oppress You

In addition to fighting or running away from danger, human beings have invented a third option: they sometimes join their oppressors, thereby eliminating the danger and excruciating anxiety accompanying it.

Something unusual happens when danger is of horrendous dimensions, beyond the experiences of most mortals, as in the case of someone who is kidnapped, treated with degradation and threatened repeatedly with death. This individual may quickly lose the capacity for realistic, normal judgments and identify with the kidnappers, viewing all others as enemies.

Becoming "cooperatively" one of them reduces otherwise unbearable anxiety and fear that could result in a much deeper, longer lasting pathological break with reality, such as schizophrenia.

Most of us, however, do not face such immediate, direct, overpowering threats to personal and physical safety. Rather, we suffer subtle sabotage of self esteem on a long-term basis, year-in, year-out. Resentment toward our oppressors builds up gradually, as do disguised defenses erected to protect ourselves.

Your Oppressors Are Human

A long time ago you found, probably much to your dismay at the time, that people are changeable. They're subject to their own needs, fatigue, fears, guilt and anxiety, all of which makes them unpredictable. At times they distort, are prejudiced, have biases, misjudge and are controlled by their unconscious selves. When you depend on them to say that you're lovable, you're also depending on their whims, judgments, physical health, fatigue, and the status of self esteem. You place yourself in a precarious, unsafe position, which, aware of it or not, leaves you anxious.

It is the human condition that when someone becomes a source of anxiety to you, your resentment begins to breed. Your greatest day-in, day-out threat to self esteem can be found in the need to have right answers. It is here, therefore, that your largest source of resentment can be found.

YOU ALWAYS EXPRESS YOUR RESENTMENT

Your resentment isn't content to sit quietly in the deep chambers of your unconscious self. No sooner do you bury it than it immediately demands to get out. It always wins, always gets its way. In one way or another you express it.

Your Own Body As a Target

Nearly everyone starts life with body parts working. Lungs, heart and circulatory system, skin, bones, eyes, ears, pancreas, bowels, bladder, sexual system, and the rest start functioning pretty much trouble-free. As you enter childhood, teenage years and adulthood, *self* has more and more impact on your body.

As long as you feel valued, maintain self esteem and are free of having to be right, your body will, with some exceptions, work free of disease. Only the most communicable diseases can make in-roads on your health. Even in these cases, however, there's reason to believe that resistance to highly contagious infections and ability to recover from them are influenced by your level of self esteem.

Threats to how you feel about yourself trigger resentment toward those who make you feel this way. Unless self esteem is restored, resentment grows progressively into anger, then hate and, finally, rage. The *resentment to rage* sequence, if not expressed openly at the conscious level, expresses itself covertly against the organs of your body. It is inevitable.

YOU ARE YOUR PRODUCTS

We are much more convinced that we exist by evidence that we *affect* somebody or something, and by our feelings rather than our thoughts.[7]

Roderic Gorney

The Human Agenda

Dr. Gorney's statement tells us that you become aware that you are an identity, that you exist, by the fact you affect others; and the way you affect them is experienced powerfully through your feelings. Having an impact on other people and experiencing this emotionally has far more meaning for you than your thoughts have.

It is, in fact, the remnants of your ancient feelings, long since forgotten at the conscious level, that affect what thoughts you have today. Many of these feelings, those that influence you most, have to do with Early Mother who abandoned you after your first year and a half of life.

The Shock of Later Mother Replacing Your Early Mother

As the days and weeks passed you became aware that your products were an expression of who you were. They reflected your uniqueness, your identity, your person. You could be identified by others by what you did, by the ways you thought, felt and acted. In fact, you began to recognize yourself, know who you were, by these products. You and your products became one and this would never change.

If, for example, you use profanity, this behavior becomes a part of you. It's a piece of your identity. You are partly known by it, identified by its use. You're someone who uses profane words.

On the other hand, if you don't use profanity, this also is who you are. You're identified partly as someone who doesn't use profane language.

The only way you can get separated from your products is to become a vegetable. Do nothing. Have no thoughts or feelings; don't act at all. So it is that you ARE your products and your potential products.

When someone says, "I'm not mad at you, but at what you did," this is nonsense. If you hadn't existed, what you did wouldn't have happened. You're responsible for your behavior. Whatever else they tell you, you are what you do, and their anger is directed at your person.

When Early Mother tried to get you to change your behavior, you didn't feel as acceptable as in the past. You got the impression that something — you — were wrong. Those efforts to control you linger on. Vague, dimly remembered feelings of unacceptability continue to live actively in your unconscious self. Though hidden from awareness ancient memories of having to change your behavior in order to win her smiles and relaxed approval still determine much of how you respond to yourself and others.

NICE PERSONS ARE APT TO DIE EARLY

Buying Self Esteem with Good Behavior Products

Trying to be good and nice has become a way of life. It seems to make sense since this is how you win self esteem and love. When you're otherwise smiles disappear from faces. Your value dips and rewards are frozen. The marketplace of people with love for sale thins out. Only when you return to producing their kind of right products can your stock soar again. Sell yourself on their terms, whatever the market demands, and they'll hand out affection that you must have in order to live.

Recognizing a Nice Person

The individual identified as "nice" is one who time and again is pointed out as good natured and always even-tempered. People have difficulty recalling this person's becoming irritated. Whatever the circumstances, the nice person holds feelings inside, usually burying them deeply beyond anyone's awareness.

On the other hand, the so-called actualized, fully functioning person is one who not only lives mostly according to society's rules, but who can, when provoked, become defensively irritated, upset, and downright mad.

More often than not individuals who are said to be "nice, good people" are not fully functioning, and are nice at a considerable expense to personal and physical well-being. They can't express much of who they are. Easy access to deeper feelings and ideas is unavailable to them. Cautious souls, careful not to offend, they hope for the slightest acceptance. In avoiding behavior that might be criticized, they sacrifice spontaneity.

Being the Model Child

Among the many requirements of the model child is that of not disturbing others. Be nice. Put aside your own wishes. Deny your needs. Be quiet, subservient, unobtrusive. Live in the shadows. Stay out of the spotlight. Blend into the woodwork. Don't disrupt. The model child works overtime at having the right kind of thoughts, feelings, answers and other behavior. Uniqueness, creativity and refreshing spontaneity are sacrificed for approval.

In hospitals, model patients who take great pains to please parent-figures (nurses and doctors), have a higher death rate than do complaining patients who are more difficult to manage. When model patients do escape death, they're more likely to return to the hospital on other occasions, as if trying to die. Rather than disturb a nurse by touching a button, they prefer to suffer through the night.[8] They follow the doctor's orders strictly. However awful the food they don't complain. They sacrifice their own needs, avoid venting feelings, but the frustration takes its toll on their bodies. Their only reward is the satisfaction that they are considered good persons, worthy of love. Once again they've avoided losing self esteem, pathetically and needlessly sacrificing themselves for a few temporary morsels of feeling all right about themselves.

"Nice" and "Good" People More Apt to Get Cancer and Die Earlier

Holding feelings back doesn't fit the way you're made. Being the sort of person others want you to be simply to win approval can cost you your life. Literally.

Psychologists examined 160 women who were thought to possibly have breast cancer.[9] After medical study it was found that 69 did, in fact, have cancer. Physicians then examined results of the earlier psychological studies. They found that 66 percent of the women with cancer had bottled up their feelings. They repressed, *beyond their own awareness,* their hostile, aggressive impulses to lash out at others. However, only half as many cancer-free women, 33 percent, couldn't face their own anger.

Cancer Victims More Likely To Bury Their Anger

The most repressed emotion of these cancer patients was anger. Psychiatrist Greer reported, "Never, or not more than once or twice in their adult lives, have they openly shown anger."

Two other physicians, Drs. Alexander and Cutler, studied still another 40 women with breast cancer. They found these victims to be essentially the same kind of *person.*[10] They buried their rage and were unaware of being angry at all. Their lesson had been learned well. "Be a good person, don't be stubborn or demanding, think right thoughts and behave in right sorts of ways."

Further, it was found that these women suffered an unfulfilled, non-trusting, obligating relationship with their mothers. Ignoring their own feelings and needs, they became the self-sacrificing daughter, offering themselves on the sacrificial altar of being right and dutiful, "like mother wants me to be if I'm to be lovable."

Unknown to themselves, this indentureship paralyzed their spontaneity. They hid their resentment behind a facade of being nice, good, pleasant. Eventually their buried anger gnawed away not only at happiness but their own breasts, symbols of motherness.

In addition, when these women slammed the door on their anger, other feelings were closed off. Nearly all were sexually inhibited. Passively, in disguised ways, they rejected their mothers by being apathetic toward becoming a mother themselves.

In the end, of course, these women paid a horrendous price for being *nice,* burying their angry feelings. They surrendered fulfillment of sexual expression. Enjoyment of mothering was lost. For many the cost was life itself.

Obviously, many women who contract breast cancer have had adequate mothering. They've been able to express feelings, have satisfying sexual experience and enjoy mothering. Yet evidence mounts suggesting a need for a no-strings-attached way of loving, making it possible to trust your own feelings, whatever they might be. This is possible. You can discover love without having to be good, and in the process your resentment melts away. When you're angry you can face it, accept it, and share it in non-destructive ways, either to others or yourself. Anger that's recognized as a normal emotion, not something you must be ashamed and frightened of, won't hurt you or anyone you love. Only when feeling guilty about your anger, frightened of its consequences, can it become a problem and destructively exceed its otherwise normal boundaries.

In Nancy Friday's book, *My Mother/My Self* (which likely has liberated more women than any other single book during the seventies) she reminds us of the critical need for separating one's self from your early bonds. Only then can you give life to yourself and those you love.[11] A full life becomes possible only when experiencing self esteem and love without first burying it at a cost to yourself.

You Get Sick of Pleasing Others, Literally

Over a long period of time autopsies were performed on men and women who had died for reasons other than cancer.[12] Of men over 50, 45 percent were found to have a cancerous prostate. Yet there was no evidence of the cancer having been activated. If this percentage holds up it would mean that out of every 100 men over age 50 reading this book, 45 of you have a cancerous prostate gland. And a bunch of you under age 50, though not diagnosed, also have cancer.

The question is, why isn't the cancer that lives in these men running wild and destroying them? What is the trigger that makes cancer cells deadly? Dr. Philip West,[13] in studies of women with cancer symptoms, reports that it's possible everyone has had or will have cancer but never know it. They'll likely die much later of altogether different illnesses. Again the question: if cancer cells are a part of us all, why does the cancer consume some persons while others escape it?

Buried Feelings Bury Cancer Patients

A method of predicting how long a new cancer patient can be expected to live has been developed by Dr. Bruno Klopfer.[14] The patient is asked to describe what is seen in meaningless globs of splattered ink, the Rorschach test. Other than knowing the type of cancer afflicting the patient, no additional information is needed.

Dr. Klopfer has found that persons who spend a great deal of effort trying to be, as he says, "good and loyal" within expectations of the world die quickly. They use themselves up, so to speak, draining their energy in an effort to be the kind of person that will escape criticism. They try desperately to live their lives beyond reproach. As a result, not much of self and body is left guarded from cancer cells ready to multiply and take over. These "good and loyal" patients, Dr. Klopfer found, were unable to get well or even live an average cancer expectancy period.

On the other hand people who spend little of themselves trying to please others, who spontaneously share feelings, live beyond the expected period of time.

PROMISES OF PRAISE,
THREATS OF PUNISHMENTS

Few of Mentally Ill Die of Cancer

Studies in four countries have indicated that mentally ill patients seldom die of cancer. Death from cancer in people *without* a mental illness is nearly 70 percent more frequent than among psychotic patients.[15] This fits Dr. Klopfer's findings. The psychotic person has stopped working overtime being loyal to the reality of pleasing others and fitting into society. This person has pulled out of what society has defined as "reality," a system of controlling people with promises of praise and threats of punishment. The psychotic or disordered patient has designed a way of thinking that makes it unnecessary to defend against being the wrong kind of person. This logic system differs from people who react with right kinds of behavior done in hopes of winning self esteem.

BECOMING PAVLOV'S DOG, SKINNER'S PIGEON

At school, you found yourself set up like Pavlov's salivating dogs or caged like Skinner's pecking pigeons. When you produced correct responses, got all your Friday spelling test words right, you were rewarded. The rewarding pellets were gold stars, happy faces stamped on your paper, 100% written in large, red numerals, and teacher's smiles. These became signals that you were all right as a person. When you didn't perform like Pavlov's dogs or Liddle's goats, your self esteem was shocked. The electric pain sent through your self-picture may have been administered with a "D" or "F" letter grade, a frown or other kinds of punishments.

Later, you may have been in a classroom where the teacher used a more humane form of molding you. Like Skinner's pigeons, if you performed as the teacher required, you were rewarded. When you failed to meet the teacher's goals, the only pain was "no reward" at all. No attention, a kind of indifference, *was given* to you. "No reward" for your product was more humane than shocking you with an "F" label.

Yet the question always left painfully somewhere deep inside you was:

> But where is my reward this time? Billy is getting a gold
> star and smiles. Where are mine?

The absence of reward became a loss, a punishment. This behavior modification way of controlling you was subtle and though disguised, it had the same devastating results. You were convinced that:

> I must perform like the teacher wants me to, in order to be
> rewarded. I must surrender my sense of autonomy, sub-
> merge my self below the surface in order to be valued.

In your first five years at home you became well-grounded in the importance of being right, not wrong, and good, not bad. It remained for the schools, however, to take what little sense of independence and self esteem which you had left, and systematically reduce you to Pavlov's dog or, in a more modern school, to Skinner's pigeon. As both Pavlovian and Skinnerian types of teachers disregard the newer, more advanced layers of brain tissues that human beings have, teaching you as they would teach animals, they lay waste to countless millions of lives each year, around the world.

All day long, day-in, day-out, you were moved from one animal training act to the other, making a circus of what are called schools. You discovered that wrong responses somehow meant that you were a bad person. Then there were always those nagging labels to prove it: "F," "D" and "C-"; unhappy faces stamped on your papers, large, red check marks showing where you had been wrong. For the typical "A"

student, a "B" always loomed as possibly just around the corner —
"B" standing for B-A-D, and a loss of self esteem.

Devised to control you, these marks on your products became
labels on your person. Resentment began to grow. In time, anger was
generated and boiled into rage, rage that they told you was wrong.
Whatever you were told about it, your rage had to be expressed
toward people, often in disguises or symbolic behavior. When you
couldn't turn against them, its acid began to eat away at some part of
your body, making you sick.

YESTERDAY'S CHILDHOOD IS TODAY'S SOCIETY

"If I fail in what I do, I fail in what I am."

From a suicide note by Amy, age 15[16]

As young people complete their first 15 or 16 years in a society that
demands them to produce right and good products, we find them
carrying great burdens of anger, even rage. Many who are unable to
disguise their anger strike out at the world or themselves. Hidden
deeply in their unconscious selves is the unbearable wish to destroy
loved ones. In order to protect others they turn their rage inward, destroying themselves. Each day in America 30 teenagers commit
suicide.[17]

In addition, many others who have lived their first 20 years under a
right-wrong, good-bad control system are in such pain that they separate themselves from reality, with more than half the patients in
mental hospitals being under age 21.

Some strike directly at society. More serious crimes against persons and property are committed by 15-year-olds than any one other
age group; 16-year-olds have nearly as many arrests.[18] While more 15-

and 16-year-olds are arrested than any other age group, it's more accurate to say that 15- and 16-year-olds get *caught* in their crimes more than any other age group.

Earning self esteem with right answers affects everyone. Most people have at some time angrily struck out at the world they live in. The National Crime Commission, for example, found that 91 of every 100 people studied admitted that they had done something which would have sent them to jail had they been caught.

Most Direct Form of Expressing Rage: Murder

Finally, there are those who express anger directly, in its most brutal form. They murder. Between 1970 and 1974, one of every 10,000 Americans was murdered. This was more than the number killed on battlefields of the Viet Nam War.[19] Every 26 minutes someone is murdered in the UnitedStates.[20]

Occasionally the morning paper reader is shocked to read that the community's "model teenager," "the perfect kid" murdered his family. Chances are he spent childhood and early teens being right, exceptionally good, to please others. Trading right answers for signs of respect cost others their lives. Floodgates holding back his silent, unknown rage suddenly opened, sweeping over him and the gate-keepers of his existence.

ANGRY SOCIETY STRIKES BACK AT ITSELF

Ways that are used with children, teenagers and adults in order to shape a desirable, healthy society aren't working! An army of one-half million police officers are patrolling America. As you are reading these words, one-half million persons are locked behind bars. Nearly a million more are checked regularly by probation officers, protecting you from further attack.

Twelve million serious crimes are committed each year in America.[21] You live in a world where, every hour of the day, there are:

6 women raped
52 individuals robbed
112 vehicles stolen
360 burglaries
720 larcenies[22]

In all, every 60 seconds 21 serious crimes are committed. Among those reported each year are:

56,000 rapes
(51 of every 100,000 women and girls)
21,000 murders
500,000 aggravated assaults with a gun
3,500,000 burglaries ($1.4 billion loss)
500,000 robberies ($154 million loss)
900,000 auto thefts

Furthermore, the Starnes report of a Justice Department study said that 50 percent of crimes go unreported.

While many points can be argued in this book, what cannot be denied is that society's chief method of shaping us is to use praise and award status, affection and love when our behavior fits its current definition of what's right and good. Payment is not always directly in words, but often awarded through symbols that tell us that we've been good. Special privileges, promotions and a host of other signs have been invented to signify that we've been right and good.

When we don't produce, when we don't do what's expected, withdrawal of these benefits is made, or, worse, we are punished. Punishment may include direct verbal abuse, rejection, or physical pain. In our schools, the scarlet letter "F" is among the worst indignities fastened around the necks of children and teenagers.

Eons ago, organisms that failed to develop a rage center became extinct. When they were attacked they simply didn't survive. Eventually they became extinct, almost passively annihilated.

YOUR RAGE CENTER

Somewhere near the center of your head you have a *rage center*. It's neither bad nor good. It's there to protect you. When your person or body is in danger, your *idea brain* sizes the situation up and, automatically, sends a message to your *feeling brain*. The nature of the message—in this case danger—determines which part of your feeling brain will receive it. Danger messages create all kinds of reactions in your head and body. In particular such messages always trigger the part of your feeling brain that we call your rage center. When it's tripped into action you're prepared to be aggressive, even attack. Without this center you couldn't become sufficiently angry to protect yourself.

Getting In Touch With Your Rage Center

If you were to open up your head and touch your rage center you would attack the nearest person, even though not having been threatened or endangered.[23,24]

Stimulate an animal's rage center and it, also, even though not provoked, will attack. If no animal or person is present, it will attack an object, such as a tennis ball. Touch its rage center and it'll attack large, ferocious animals that it would ordinarily avoid.

One woman whose rage center was stimulated became instantly angry, threatening the experimenter. When the stimulation to her rage center was turned off, her hostile attitude disappeared.[25]

Unlike the period of cavedwellers, human beings today are seldom attacked by wild animals stalking in the underbrush. In our complex, controlled society A DISAPPROVING GLANCE, ATTITUDE, OPINION, AND — ESPECIALLY — WITHDRAWAL OF LOVE BECOME ATTACKS UPON YOUR PERSON. When you live life by trying to win approval and love through producing the right products, you place your happiness, self esteem and eventually the health of your body in a hazardous position.

Danger of Depending on Others
to Label You "Right" and "Good"

The whims of others, their fluctuating states of accepting or rejecting you often based on their own need for self esteem, determine how you feel about yourself. Giving this power to them, you buy into a precarious arrangement. When you must be the right kind of person based on their standards, you experience a sense of danger. This human judgment of your personal behavior always has in it the potential danger of lost self esteem. Being endangered by your right-wrong kind of evaluators, you resent them.

The danger and painful anxiety from this sort of dependency get registered in your *idea brain.* The instant this happens your ideas trigger one of the areas of your *feeling brain,* in this case your rage center. Your impulse is to strike out at whoever makes you dependent on their "rights" and "goods."

The moment you want to hit at someone, whether with words or fists, you know that such behavior would be criticized. Fearful of being wrong and bad, you hold your anger in reserve. Guiltily you send it deep into your unconscious self, where you no longer are aware that it exists.

But it does exist. Eventually it'll be released, often in disguised forms that you and others don't recognize, sabotaging an intimate relationship. On the other hand, you may turn your rage against an organ of your body, getting sick.

All Animal Life Requires Independence

Humankind is not alone in its need to be free from the control of others. Monkeys, rats, cats and other lower animals are driven to be free of their masters. Dogs will bury their leashes or chew them to shreds.[26]

If an animal is forced to run on an activity wheel which has little steps on it and a motor driving it around on its axle, it'll instantly turn the motor off. The animal resists running on a wheel set in motion by someone else. Whether aware of it or not, you also do this in your relationships with people. In subtle, sometimes direct ways you resist their efforts to set you in motion, spinning your life in the direction of their "goods" and "rights." Human negativism, because of moralistic efforts to control behavior, is a critical part of most relationships, in work, play and intimacy.

On the other hand, if the animal itself turns on the motor and the experimenter turns it off, the animal will immediately turn the motor back on. These remarkable experiments by Dr. Kavanu[27] have shown that we humans are not alone in our resistance to the control of our lives by others.

Certain experiments were also done with animals who, by nature, sleep during the day and are active at night. Every once in awhile the experimenter turned the dimmer switch on to full intensity. Each time this happened, the animal pressed a pedal that turned the light fully off.

However, if the light was on and the experimenter turned it off, the animal frequently turned it back on to full intensity. This resistance to being controlled continued for many weeks. Only much later will it press the switch to a dim level that, by nature, it prefers.

Lowly Worm Resists Being Controlled

Even the ancient, primordial planarian worm seems to require a sense of being in control of its own destiny. Planaria are so small that when five average-size planaria are lined up in a row, about five of them are needed to form a line merely one inch long. These worms have a structure so simple that not until the electronic microscope was invented could it be certain that they have a central nervous system.

While no more evolved than they were during the dinosaur period, these hardly visible creatures can learn to conduct themselves in ways that literally save their lives. If, for example, food is withheld from planaria until they're desperately hungry, they can learn to make turns in a maze that lead to food, saving themselves from starvation. Their reward for doing the "right, expected behavior" is life itself.

Finally, though, when the worms' learning efficiency reaches its peak, they suddenly refuse to be manipulated any longer. Apparently preferring death to strict, arbitrary control over their lives, they refuse to run the maze.[28]

You Become Angry When Made to Run Mazes

You learned early that life is made up of mazes constructed by other people for you to run. As long as your maze-running behavior pleases them, you're rewarded. They smile, admire you and offer other prizes.

You pay a heavy price for these rewards. Harvard psychologist Dr. Jerome Bruner tells us that the person "holds back, or strikes out compulsively, or is shamed by the power that others have."[29] Surrendering your freedom, giving away your rights and trying to fit expectations of others ends in personal and physical destruction.

Disaster of Behavior Modification

Behavior modification is a system used by people to change you. They wait until you live up to their expectations and then reward you for it. You're told in some way or another that what you've done has been right or good, so that you feel all right about yourself. This Skinnerian method of controlling people, as it's sometimes called, is occasionally used to treat mentally disordered persons, such as schizophrenics. They're rewarded with praise, prizes and privileges when they change their behavior in desirable ways. The results can be dramatic. They sometimes show marked improvement, seeming to start their journey toward getting well.

In time, however, they suffer a reversal, deteriorating into a more severe state of mental disorder than before. Dr. Silvano Arieti, the world's foremost authority on schizophrenia, reports that the schizophrenic who is treated in this way eventually gets sicker, "perhaps because he has experienced yet another attack on his freedom and dignity." [30]

I've made similar observations with students in schools who've made initial, rapid progress in learning when behavior modification is used. Later, however much the early gains may have been, they begin to go downhill. In one way or another they suffer severe consequences of having sold out to the sound of the teacher's song of "that's right, that's good." Emotionally and physically they pay an exorbitant price.

Little wonder that much of what you learned in school was soon forgotten "after the test." Learning for rewards of feeling right about yourself is learning that's short-lived. It's an affront to your freedom and dignity. It's so painful that you put the experience behind you, in the regions of your unconscious. Its remnants are there, however, embroidered in the resentment of your mind. Yet they offered you little else for nourishing your self esteem. You became dependent on morsels of praise thrown to you when producing their kind of product in their expected ways.

Destructive as it is, this remains the universal way of getting people to learn, become constructive citizens, raise children, and have intimate relationships. This "way" seems to make sense. Saying "right" or "good" to people makes them feel O.K. about themselves, at least for the moment. This sort of reward, it appears, will get people to repeat their desirable behavior. What could possibly be destructive about this method?

After having been told that "you did it right, did it good," at the bottom of your self-satisfied feeling, usually beyond immediate awareness, a deeper, more significant feeling occurs. It is true, of course, that when first being rewarded with a "that's good!" you feel safe. You're not being criticized. Smiles, words or other forms of expressing pleasure about your product lets you know that for the moment, all is well. You haven't lost self esteem. At the same time, however, a part of you knows, even though only dimly sensed, that had your product not measured up to their standards of right and good, you would have been devalued. At best there would have been no rewards indicating that you were an acceptable, right sort of good person. Placed in this bind, living in the shadows of those who control your self esteem, you begin to resent them. Resentment, conscious of it or not, becomes the feeling which, more than any other, influences how you feel about yourself in the product-centered world surrounding you.

Without Rewards You Die

Let me say emphatically that rewards aren't to be undervalued. They're indispensable. People learn only as a result of being rewarded.

The question, therefore, has nothing to do with whether rewards are useful or destructive. Instead, what is to be answered is "what *kinds* of rewards should be given?" Further, how are they to be offered and what meanings are to be attached to them? Answers to these questions, more than anything, influence your self esteem, relationships with people, intimacy, satisfaction and physical health. Also affected is how well you learn, whether in or out of school.

As long as you continue to trade being right and good for tidbits of short-lived self esteem, you'll be resentful and angry. This anger itself won't interfere with your well-being nor make you sick. How you feel *about* your anger (frightened of it, ashamed, guilty) and hiding it from yourself in deep regions of the unconscious part of you, this is what impairs your personal relationships and body. In the pages that follow, more and more we'll see how this works, why it is that, in fearfully and guiltily hiding your feelings, you cannot win.

Fear and Guilt About Sex
Running Second to Hate Feelings

During the Victorian era people were more frightened and ashamed of their sexual feelings than of any other. For the past quarter century this has been changing. Today, it's the person's own feelings of anger that are the most anxiety-provoking.

You've been taught since early childhood that angry feelings are dangerous and bad and should be avoided at all costs. When 3,000 teachers took a word association test (FWAT) designed to tap their buried feelings, it was found that more than anything else, they were frightened and ashamed of their resentment and hate feelings.[31] Dr. Anne MacLean, using the same test, found that teachers are more fearful of their hate feelings than sexual feelings.[32] They bury, beyond awareness, feelings that have to do with resentment, hate, anger and rage.

This is in contrast, of course, to what's generally thought. Since Freud, at least, it's been believed that people are more reluctant to face their sexual feelings than hate feelings, that guilt and shame about sexual thoughts caused them the most trouble. This may have been true in Victorian times, when Freud lived, but it doesn't seem to be the case today.

When you bury feelings far from your awareness it's said that you're *repressing* part of yourself. Because society has taught you that you're not likely to be loved when you have certain thoughts and feelings, you repress large parts of who you are.

Supressing and Repressing

When you have thoughts or feelings that you are aware of but don't express, you're said to be *supressing* them. When you suppress what you'd like to say, it may be uncomfortable. It might also, at times, interfere with your moods, leaving you irritable, upset and unhappy. However, keeping such ideas and feelings in your conscious mind, you're not likely to get into deep emotional trouble nor have your body suffer unnecessary illness.

For some reason, being mindful of feelings, whatever they might be — however angry and sexual — they do not ordinarily lead to undue suffering. You recognize them, see them for what they are and have a sense of being in control of them and your life.

On the other hand, you're also put together in ways that when certain thoughts are deeply disturbing to you, you hide them in your unconscious self. You repress them. Repressed ideas and feelings differ from suppressed ones, then, in that you don't know you have them.

Yet they control you. From behind the scenes of your conscious self, they relentlessly direct your daytime behavior and become material for your nocturnal dreams.

There's value in repressing painful, frightening thoughts. Hidden in your unconscious, these ideas are less capable of flooding you with anxiety and guilt. In the long run, however, repressed thoughts eat away at your self esteem. Love relationships suffer, feelings of intimacy and erotic behavior are gnawed away, and eventually your body suffers ill health.

Tyranny of Right and Good

At every age, from the so-called "terrible twos" through rebellious teenage years and into adulthood, you struggle for independence from authority's power to praise and belittle you. History presents a picture of blatant forms that authority has used against humankind, as in the case of dictatorships. Prejudice is still another oppressive tool in the hands of certain cliques, some religious organizations, cultures and political institutions.

A more subtle, pervasive form of tyranny attempts to control people with praise. It's your human right to be imperfect and, at the same time, be loved as you are. Beyond dictatorships there's no greater tyranny than controlling through the threat of taking away your self esteem when you're not the good, perfect person they expect. The moment you agree, consciously or not, to get your self esteem by trying to do the right thing, pleasing others as a way of getting their praise, you've joined the oppressed. You're no longer free.

Your Resentment at Having to Be Right

Not only you but also animals strike out furiously at the world when threatened with having to behave in right ways in order to feel a sense of safety. One scientist, Dr. Arizin, found that animals would attack if they had been receiving rewards and were cut off from the supply. They would strike out at anyone present, including family members. If no one was available, animals would attack a stuffed object.[33]

How familiar this scene is among humankind! The beloved child feeling thwarted by a newborn brother or sister. A husband feeling slighted at a party or, for that matter, in his own home. In-laws feeling that they don't get enough time and attention. The child who isn't chosen by the teacher to clean the chalkboard. Office workers and teachers feeling bypassed when commendations or promotions are passed out.

You Prefer to Run Away

When self esteem is threatened you immediately become aggressive and want to attack but usually don't. Attacking those you love who diminish your self esteem seems dangerous. You may be retaliated against with even more vicious attacks on your personal worth, possibly being rejected altogether.

Consequently, you choose a safer defense, withdrawal. You become cautious about sharing ideas in class, fearful of being wrong. You may hold back deeper, personal feelings, afraid to risk yourself, anxious that this may open the door to criticism. You hide your political opinions, views on art, athletics and life.

Rather than expose yourself to potential criticism, you begin to view your thoughts as being of little value, uninteresting to others. You dissolve the image of yourself as being attractive, withdraw into cautious behavior, pulling back from delightful spontaneity that you're capable of expressing.

You Are Not Alone

Withdrawing from hostile experiences is so common among humankind that books are written about it. And it's not limited to humankind. The animal world has a general preference for running away, not wishing to risk head-on attacks.

Monkeys, when given pain and the option of fleeing or attacking, prefer to run away.[34] Wild creatures of the jungle don't typically attack when in danger; they retreat. And so do you.

While losing self esteem and love, you're required, for the most part, to remain in the setting—job, marriage, family, school—where you experience this pain. Fearful of lashing out, you can only retreat. Often there's no place to go except withdraw into yourself.

It is here, when you contain your resentment inside, that it begins to eat away at your happiness. Cells, tissues and organs of your body can no longer endure. They become sick. It doesn't have to be this way.

PART THREE

YOUR FEELINGS
SPEAK THROUGH
YOUR BODY

ARE YOU SICK ABOUT YOURSELF?

If you are, you're not alone. More than 50 of every 100 persons who enter doctors' offices with a physical disorder, disease or need for surgery *wouldn't be there were it not for their feelings about themselves.*[35,36]

The sickness is real. There may be a fever or pain, a need for surgery. It's NOT in their imagination! Yet, were it not for negative feelings about self, illness wouldn't have occurred in the first place.

Feelings of aloneness, separation from important love relationships, loss of self esteem and most of all, rage, turn against the body. Physiology of the body, its blood and chemistry, tissues and cells, change. Equilibrium — balance between feelings, ideas and body processes — breaks down. When self-rejecting feelings take over, self destroys self.

Loss of self esteem, feelings of inadequacy, sense of failure, and deeply submerged rage about what others have done to you may end in amputation of an important part of who you are.

Your self image is one of a person who is merely tolerated, worn, ragged, empty and unwanted. Your reaction to this is rage that, like a seething, restless volcano churning deep inside, is ready to spend its fury onto the world.

YOU HURT MORE THAN YOU SHOULD

When you live every day on product-centered love, eventually it takes its toll. You begin to hurt far more than you should. Some persons hurt more than others. Many despair, and in one way or another a majority destroy themselves.

For most, self-destruction is slow, insidious. Ultimate annihilation of self is hidden even from the person bent upon dying. Unknown to themselves they turn their wrath inward. Some use illnesses, others fail at their jobs, destroy their marriages, tear apart friendships, lose when winning would be easier. In one way or another they manage to be miserable. Personal and physical deterioration follows and they become candidates for sickness, organs that stop working, and early death.

One Tries to Die Every Minute

Every minute of each 24-hour day, someone's anguish is so intense that an attempt is made to commit suicide.[37] Every 24 minutes someone succeeds in this final act of struggling from the control of others.

More Americans die each year by their own hand than those who succumb to all infectious diseases combined.[38] But rage turned in on self isn't limited to Americans. Each year more than 15,000 Canadians attempt suicide, with 1,700 actually dying.[39] Around the world every year several million individuals try to kill themselves. One-half million of these succeed. The World Health Organization tells us that suicide is among the planet earth's ten most frequent causes of death.[40]

Dying to Be Nice to Others

Rather than lash out murderously at society, particularly at those who have given love to them as a reward for being right and good, these individuals annihilate themselves. They protect loved ones that enrage them.[41] Suicide is murder turned inward. Freud missed on this one. Unlike what he thought, especially at one period, there is no death instinct, no drive to destroy one's self. On the contrary, it's the need to protect one's own concept of self, keep intact the picture the individual has of being someone who would not destroy a loved person, that leads to suicide. "In order to protect others and the picture I have of myself, I turn my rage inward, eliminate myself.' All of life, your every act, is to maintain and embellish who you are. Sometimes, however, indeed often these efforts are born of ways that, unknown to you, in the long run work against your welfare.

The suicidal act is intended to aid individuals to break free of the bondage that right and good create. It takes them beyond criticism and praise of their masters, beyond their rage, into death. They leave behind only guilt and mourning in those who cared and might have loved on a different basis.

BEING "NICE" AND "GOOD": PRODUCTS THAT END IN SELF-DESTRUCTION

There are those who, in order to feel a sense of personal worth, live so totally by the book of rules that they sacrifice spontaneity. They're afraid to risk much, if any, of their impulse life. Cautiously they think before acting or speaking out, even when the occasion doesn't call for cumbersome deliberation.

These individuals are super-careful not to break the least significant rule. They follow rules even when a particular one may not apply. They can't risk being wrong, bad or criticized. Often these persons are referred to as *nice*. They're beyond reproach, never criticized, always predictable. They're also colorless, insipid and seldom known for their humor. They're nice but pay a high price in trying to please others.

"Nice" Children Can Expect To Live Shorter Lives

Nowhere in the world, perhaps, can "nicer" children be found than in Denmark. At the same time, for 100 years Denmark has continued to watch its children grow up into a population with one of the world's highest suicide rates.[42] And nowhere are children so seldom given love without first giving right answers and being good.

Second to Denmark, another Scandinavian country, Sweden, has

75

the highest suicide rate. Here, as well, children are unusually "nice." Danish and Swedish children are far "better behaved" than American children.

How are Danish and Swedish children reared? When the Danish child's behavior fails to be the kind of product expected by parents, a profound sense of guilt is foisted onto the child. Psychiatrist Hendin points out that the child is left to feel that mama has been hurt; you let her down; she's deeply unhappy.

When mother leaves the child feeling painfully guilty, this stirs anger that the child must hide, even from self. There's no tolerance for anger toward the family. Sweden's problem with its own rage is reflected in all kinds of ways. In July, 1979, laws were enacted that prohibit parents from humiliating children as a way of disciplining. Physical punishment is forbidden.[43] The laws seem, on the one hand, to reflect an effort to control inner rage that might get out of control and, on the other, but simply another expression of the need to be "good" and not punish others.

As in the case of Swedish children, the Danish child is made to feel unloved whenever failing to achieve at high levels. Emphasis is on being the best, producing high quality products in order to win love. It is here, in loving children in impact-centered ways rather than product-centered ones, that changes in Sweden's parental behavior can have the healthy, facilitating effects they seem to want. Legislation against punishment, a negative effort at best, can only increase anger and the need to lash out at helpless ones and, eventually, their own selves.

Spontaneity of the Swedish child is frowned on. Instead, reason, logic, in fact all matters of the intellect are what's exhalted. Ideas are viewed as respectable, feelings disrespected. Self esteem is won when exercising the intellect, lost while showing emotions. As might be guessed, more than anywhere else, Swedish males are criticized for crying.

Denmark, with its emphasis on winning love and reputation for having nice children, has a suicide rate 100 percent higher than the United States. In Sweden, where children spend their days trying to be nice in order to win respect, the rate is 70 percent greater than in American and Canadian families.

"Nice" People Are Passive, Dependent Persons

While Danish children are nice, they're also passive and dependent. They have little confidence in their own solutions, depending on others for approval rather than finding it in themselves. Demands for being right and good become prison walls, limiting self-direction and spontaneity.

Less Control and Supervision: Less Suicide

Across the way, in another Scandinavian nation, Norwegian mothers respect the rights of children, even more so than in the United States. They're less compulsed to control and supervise. Norwegian children don't have to be superior. They can expect love whether or not they're "the best."

Living in a society that doesn't use praise for getting right answers and being good, Norwegians have a much lower suicide rate. In fact, compared with Norway, Denmark's suicide rate is 300 percent greater, Sweden's roughly 200 percent more, and America's 30 percent higher.

YOUR INNER ENVIRONMENTS

Your body's glands work constantly to keep things in balance. When you're threatened by losing self esteem or placed in a precarious, strings-attached position of producing the right products for other persons, these glands go into action. They try to protect you from attacks on your self-picture. At the slightest threat to self esteem dramatic changes take place inside you. Blood sugar and pressure rise, stomach acid increases, arteries tense, tighten, narrow or expand, and a host of other changes take place.

You Have Two Brains

In a way, you have two brains. One, near the middle of your head, is sometimes called the "old brain." Human beings have had this from almost the beginning, when still more animal than human. In the process of becoming more human, spread out over several million years, layer upon layer of tissue were laid on top of the old brain. Because these layers came later in evolutionary changes, they're called the new brain. It's like having a second brain. The advanced development of your new brain is what makes you different from animals.

Your old brain, along with some glands, is involved with your feelings. Today people talk about this as the "affective domain." Your new brain, on the other hand, works with ideas — ideas of all sorts, such as those that make up values, attitudes, thoughts, symbols or all kinds of intellectual behavior. It's your "cognitive domain."

Together these two brains — or domains — combine to express meanings and feelings. More than anything it's your feeling and thinking brains that direct your glands on how and where to express your feelings. How you think and feel about yourself and others has powerful effects on both happiness and your body.

HOW YOU SYMBOLIZE YOUR FEELINGS
THROUGH YOUR BODY

Wedding Finger Dermatitis

When conflict takes place between your two brains—between what you feel and what you think — stress begins to build, tension mounts. When stress becomes too painful to face you may try to hide from what it is that frightens you or creates guilt. You disguise your wishes and conflicts — the ones that make you feel lost self esteem and un-loved—expressing your stress through symbols.

You produce a symbol, or substitute product, that represents the frightening event.[44] For example, just as a wedding band on the "wedding finger" of the left hand symbolizes marriage, a band holding two persons together, you may unconsciously direct this finger to symbolize wishes, conflict or stress in the relationship. It's not uncommon for the wedding finger of both members of the relationship to swell, even "break out" in a rash. The tissue may color, as well, giving an impression that the individual has some sort of infection. This is sometimes called "ring finger dermatitis."[45]

Itching and swelling may, especially in the case of a man, spread to the symbolic middle (penis) finger, next to the ring finger. He has, in this case, expressed his yearning indirectly, symbolically, through a part of his body that, for the time, has come to represent a relationship in conflict.

Other Parts of Your Body Used to State Your Conflicts

It could be, for example, that a diseased cervix represents stress in a marital relationship; stomach problems might be traced to an infantile, child-like dependency on mother; uterine disorders might symbolize conflicts or doubts about producing babies; inflamed ovaries could conceivably reflect conflict about feminine identity.[46]

I'm convinced that every thought and feeling you have — no exceptions! — get expressed through your cells, tissues and organs. Positive and negative ones, happy and unhappy, all are translated into body processes. The positive, basically happy person's body looks and functions basically happy and healthy.

In time, negative, conflict-ridden, resentful individuals appear less healthy. Their bodies convert unhappiness into disorders. There's no escape from what you think and feel about yourself.

DO PEOPLE MAKE YOUR BLOOD PRESSURE RISE?

Being Sick at Heart Is More Deadly Than Cancer

Persons who are sick about themselves, "sick at heart," have an affliction more deadly than cancer. Of the 30 million Americans who have hypertension, 15 million are unaware of it.[47] Every year 60,000 die of high blood pressure. Another quarter million die of causes related to hypertension. Wars, cancer, auto accidents, nothing can compare to hypertension as the great killer of humankind. They die and die and die because they're heartsick about themselves. They've lost at work, in play and with love. They've lost in the eyes of others and themselves.

The "high blood pressure type" or hypertensive individual is often a person who is calm and cool in upsetting circumstances. Inside, however, fearful of angry feelings and feeling guilty about them, pressure is put on the self to hide these emotions — pressure that gets exerted on the body as the great killer, hypertension.

Nothing can be more deadly to the heart than the loss of love. Dr. James Lynch, in his remarkable book, *The Broken Heart,* says that a majority of physicians would agree that personal relationships can have measurable, even fatal effects on the heart.[48]

The Strivers Finally Strive No More

After 50 years of striving, making every effort to produce like society demands of them, one in four American men and women are defeated into the grave with hypertension. Many have done all that was asked of them in order to be accepted. They went to school and changed. They may have even gone off to college. They married the kind of man or woman that parents and society required, had children, gave them music lessons and started their college fund. They joined the right clubs, played golf (with the right people), performed appropriate social rituals, and drove the proper automobile. They had been told that were they to do all the right things they would be rewarded with pride, self esteem and happiness.

Instead, disillusioned, angry, depressed, they end up on the psychiatrist's couch [49] or with hypertension, a few steps from burying their grief and anger in a graveyard.

YOUR "FEELING BRAIN" SENDS
FAT INTO YOUR BLOOD

When you're put under stress to be like other people want you to be, your feeling brain takes deposits of fat from throughout the body and sends it into the bloodstream. Day-in, day-out stress lines artery walls with fat. Arteries begin to narrow, reducing space for blood to flow. Sometimes a hardened piece of fat breaks away and rides to the brain or heart, often resulting in heart attacks, strokes, or death.

War Against Your Self

In any one year we can expect 700,000 people to die of coronary heart attacks, either directly or indirectly related to emotional conflict about themselves. Long, drawn-out wars between nations have death lists that cannot begin to match the yearly warring of selves in America alone.

You're seldom told about the biggest, most signifiicant cause behind heart attacks. Instead, they've drawn your attention mostly to the following causes:

High cholesterol
Overweight
Smoking
Parents with heart disease
Lack of exercise
High blood pressure
Diabetes

Yet Dr. Glass has pointed out that the majority of heart attacks don't have high cholesterol levels, only a small number are hypertensive, and fewer still are diabetic.[50] He points out that since physical factors aren't enough to explain coronary deaths, researchers have turned to the emotional lives of these victims.

The Need to Prove We're All Right

A chief characteristic of coronary persons is the need to prove themselves, to achieve superior products. Though no more intelligent, they achieve more academic honors. These high driving, product-centered persons strive mightily to prove their personal worth by producing one product after another. Each is intended to be better than the last. They become a collective monument marking the grave of individual unhappiness.

When Your Heart Gets Angry

Psychiatrists Dr. William Greene[51] and Dr. George Engel,[52] in two separate studies, also found evidence that physical characteristics ordinarily thought to trigger heart attacks aren't enough to account for them. The added necessary dimension seems to be feelings. Prior to a heart attack victims were found to be sad, depressed, anxious and easily angered. Furthermore their personal lives at home and work had taken unpleasant turns. Disharmony between self and others brought their heart, indeed lives, to a dead standstill.

Are You Being Bored to Death?

Boredom is a depressant, a heavy lid dropped over feelings. Bored people are not bored at all. They're angry. All week long, week-in, week-out, they produce their products as directed. Their routines are safe, sure and provide a modicum of love. They feel like they're doing the right things, being a "good sort of person."

In this boring way of living there's little joy, spontaneity, sudden excitement and exhilarating unpredictability. It's a product-centered existence empty of payoff for you as a person. Minimum wages are paid — fleeting moments of recognition, esteem and affection. Your take-home pay is barely at survival level. You accept this pittance, however, producing their kinds of products in payment for love, because it's the only way you know.

Your boredom may be costing you more than you think. You may be boring yourself to death, literally. Day after day you find yourself in the same old routines, tied to monotonous work, daily events, unswerving marriage rituals and family relationships. In one study of 100 women telephone workers, 25 percent had 75 percent of the illnesses. It was discovered that nearly all of these illness-prone workers were bored at their work, experienced stress at home, and lived what they described as monotonous lives. Living in sadness and with little enthusiasm for people, they went about their tasks in prescribed but unfulfilling ways. They did everything right, were good persons, hoping to escape criticism and be lovable.

Deep down, they resented their methodical, closed world, its restrictions upon their spontaneity, and being loved for only a part — the surface — of who they were. As always happens, in time they began to turn their resentment against themselves, becoming ill.

PART FOUR

DEALING
WITH YOUR
PRODUCT-CENTERED
RELATIONSHIPS

> Paradoxically, the self is valued
> only for what one can accomplish.
> It is the only measure of worth
> when relationships cannot
> furnish it.
>
> Gregory Rochlin[53]

PRODUCT-CENTERED RELATIONSHIPS: WHAT ARE THEY?

It's safe to say that your life — most of it — is made up of product-centered relationships. As I mentioned before, while humankind has leaped geometrically forward in most things, the ways we relate to each other have stayed about the same. We still depend on product-centered rewards. In getting the young to learn, shaping people into citizens, controlling society, and forming love relationships, we hold out promises of telling them in one way or another that what they've done has been right or good.

When they don't produce behavior that's wanted, we punish them in one of two ways. On the one hand we may say that what they've done (or failed to do) has been wrong or bad. On the other hand we may say or do nothing, disregarding what's been done or not done.

An absence of an evaluation becomes an evaluation. "In the past, when my behavior lived up to what you wanted, you said, 'that's right' or 'that's good.' In some way or another you let me know that what I had done was acceptable and I was an acceptable person."

As a result, "Without such rewarding signs from you, I can only believe that I've been wrong, behaved badly, and am a bad person."

And so a *product-centered* relationship is one in which you depend on getting self esteem, affection and love by behaving in ways that are labeled as "right" or "good." Dependence on these kinds of rewards for self esteem is unreliable, destructive and sometimes lethal.

IMPACT RELATIONSHIPS: WHAT ARE THEY?

The most satisfactory, enduring relationship possible is given birth in a human exchange based on *sharing impact with one another, free of right and good, wrong and bad.* A relationship of this kind is its own reward. It exceeds all rewards imaginable.

When you don't have to live up to someone else's standards in order to think of yourself as being the right sort of person, the chief source of your crippling resentment disappears. Like it or not, you do resent someone who places right-wrong, good-bad judgments on your behavior, be it a friend, business associate or love partner.

Mostly, however, you're unaware of your resentment, especially during the earlier phases of a love relationship. In time, though, resentment builds. It becomes increasingly difficult to ignore.

When you feel particularly guilty and anxious about your resentment, you hold it deep inside, its deadly venom turning against some part of your body. Eventually it seeps out and in subtle or openly expressed ways begins to erode what happens between both of you.

Most of this can be avoided. Relating in impact-centered ways, accepting and loving one another as you are, free of moralistic judgments of right and wrong, you begin to share thoughts and feelings spontaneously. A closer, more intimate relationship than you ever dreamed possible develops. Mutual respect replaces distrust. Unafraid to spontaneously share all of who you are your relationship prospers.

YOUR NEED FOR
A DEEP RELATIONSHIP

A *deep relationship* is an impact-centered relationship with intimacy. The need to be touched, held and related to in intimate ways by someone who does not judge you with rights and wrongs, goods and bads, is your birthright. It became this way while you were still inside your mother's body and during the earliest months that you spent with your Early Mother. You became bonded, not necessarily to Early Mother, but to the intimacy you enjoyed with her while free of rights and wrongs, goods and bads. So it is that you spend your lifetime, not searching for Early Mother, but for intimacy, love and self esteem free of moralistic evaluations. Only inside such a relationship will you find a satisfactory level and continuation of happiness, while also enjoying physical well-being.

Losing a Deep Relationship Endangers Your Life

When you lose a deep relationship — which sooner or later happens to everyone — you enter a critical period of your life. In severe losses, such as in divorce or death, sometimes as long as two years are needed to regain balance. Only when the loss is resolved within weeks or months are your personal and physical safety assured.

Beyond this point you run a risk of becoming seriously ill, even dying. Few can survive more than two years of stress from the loss of a deep relationship. Someone who loses a close relative to death is 70 times more likely to die within a year than is true of individuals who haven't lost a loved one.[54]

USING DRUGS WHEN LOSING DEEP RELATIONSHIPS

It's easy to observe the stress of persons who have lost a deep relationship to separation, divorce or death. Not so apparent, however, is the pain of subtle day-to-day deep relationship losses. Persons inside a deep relationship relating on a product-centered basis often suffer losses that aren't obvious. Resentment at having to behave in artificial ways in order to be valued becomes camouflaged by indirect or symbolic attacks on one another. (For this reason, often what what seems to be a "deep relationship" isn't at all, but rather a product-centered one.)

These small, daily, product-centered losses accumulate, eventually taking their toll. Vulnerability to germs increases. Many get sick or eventually die of diseases that no one near them suspects were connected with product-centered love.

Anxiety as Pain

Buried resentment and rage about having to be right to be lovable doesn't remain quietly in your conscious self. It knocks at the door to your conscious self, furiously, insistently. Your fear becomes attached to possibly opening the door to your hidden feelings. Potential awareness of what you try desperately to hide from yourself frightens and produces painful anxiety inside you. Like all pain, its purpose is to warn you of danger. When a lighted match touches near your skin you pull away. Anxiety serves the same purpose.

An Anesthetic for Your Pain

Fear and guilt regarding your resentment toward a loved one is painful, yet in spite of repressing knowledge of it deep inside, you can't rid yourself of the hurt. Painful anxiety in your personal relationships leads one of every three adults to rely on a drug that temporarily reduces this pain.[55]

Americans spend more than six billion dollars a year on Valium alone. Frantically trying to lessen personal misery, a half-million Americans have become addicted to narcotics.[56]

BEER, BOOZE AND MARIJUANA: A TURN-OFF, NOT A TURN-ON

In addition to pills, millions of Americans and Canadians use alcohol regularly as a sedative. In America, the cost of alcohol abuse and its disastrous effects is 25 billion dollars yearly, in Canada two billion dollars.[57] Only heart disease, mental illness and cancer exceed the amount of pain created by alcoholism. Persons anesthetized with alcohol are responsible for overwhelming amounts of human suffering and death. Each year some 50,000 persons die in automobile accidents. Two percent of the drivers kill 50 percent of these people, and it should be noted that two percent of all persons driving cars are chronic drinkers.[58] Person sedated with alcohol make up a great bulk of drivers having accidents.

The National Institute on Alcohol Abuse and Alcoholism estimates that there are some ten million alcoholics and problem drinkers trying to reduce their emotional misery. Alcoholism is the third leading cause of death in America.[59] Each year more than 1.25 million arrests are made of persons trying to reduce personal misery through drunkenness. Far more escape attention of police officers.[60]

By the time many young people have spent a dozen years on earth, they've become unbearably anxious about themselves. With feelings of worthlessness more than they can endure, they turn to sedatives as a way of easing self-doubts. Vast numbers of teenagers, like their parents, retreat to beer weekends or other alcoholic sedatives, with more than 500,000 teenage alcoholics populating America.[61]

Another six million, while not alcoholic, sporadically use alcohol to quiet their anxiety about themselves. In addition some five million teenagers escape through marijuana, flying from pain about themselves into altered moods that get them through the day and night.

Your Friends and Loved Ones As Alcoholics

Alcoholics are with you daily, in the neighborhood, at work or school, and in your government. They come from all socioeconomic classes, cultures and races.

Among the Indian population of America, devastation of personal lives by alcohol is even more pronounced than among the rest of the nation. About 80 percent of the American Indian population is affected by alcoholism. Simply being an Indian has nothing to do with being alcoholic. It's not in the genes, not an inherited tendency. Some thirty years ago, Indian tribes, on their own initiative, had the problem of Indian alcoholism researched. Reportedly, reasons for Indian alcoholism were found to be no different than those of white Caucasians.[62] Childrearing methods that promote gross dependency on authority, with resentment toward this sort of power relationship, are at the bottom of most addiction.

Having to be "right" and thereby a "good person" to please authority and, in so doing, win self esteem, becomes the initial impetus toward becoming an alcoholic personality.

The alcoholic is a child in a grown-up body. Severe immaturity prevents this person from postponing a need to have immediate gratification through pleasure. The alcoholic has little tolerance for anxiety. Living in a world, as we do, that requires us to be right and good

— and makes these demands all day long, every day, in every kind of relationship — anxiety becomes a constant companion. Rather than coping with even slight problems, the alcoholic sends an anesthetic into the bloodstream, quieting the rage spawned by moralistic controls.

No One Is Immune to Alcoholism

No one is immune from the effects wrought by their history of dependency on product-centered love. Religious leaders, persons high in government, everyone, all are vulnerable to traumatic consequences of getting self esteem through trying to be the right, good sort of person. Nuns of the Catholic Church, for example, have been found to suffer from alcoholism at about the same rate as the public.[63]

On the other hand, persons who live life in ways that work for both society and themselves that are effective (and which *may* be labeled by society as "right" or "good"), but do so without trying to win self esteem and love, these persons can escape becoming the alcoholic personality.

One In Nine of Your Drinking Friends Is Alcoholic

Among the millions of Americans who drink, one of every nine is alcoholic. They've become addicted to quick relief from battered self esteem. Rather than coping directly with anxiety about feeling resentful toward those who require them to be right and good, 9 of every 90 drinkers ease themselves into alcoholic oblivion.

Sexual Impotence and Alcohol

Lowered self esteem, the need to perform well as a condition of lovableness, and ensuing rage lead millions of Americans to alcohol as a way of succeeding in sex. It's the most popular of all drugs used for this purpose.[64]

Resentment grows, eventually, into rage that flattens the drive for sexual release and fulfillment. Inability to have erections or exper-

ience orgasms increasingly become a problem when, either consciously or unconsciously, the person lives in resentment. Often total
sacrifice of sexual enjoyment, release of tension, and personal well-
being is the result.

Marijuana As An Anesthetic

Across America each weekday morning a multitude of people wend
their resentful, anxious way to offices, shops, factories and schools
while smoking a marijuana joint. Anxious about themselves and how
they feel about others, they flee from their raw, product-centered real-
ities. Fearful, unsure of self, they draw the smoke of THC into their
bodies, hoping to mute the rage that screams at them. They hope that
in softening reality it will somehow get them closer to the one they
love. In the end, however, it only divides them more.

THE EARLY HOPE OF MARIJUANA
WENT UP IN SMOKE

Early studies of marijuana indicated that a drug had at last been
found which would ease life's inevitable stresses, doing so without serious or even minor side effects. With the passing of time, however, a
decidedly different picture has started to come into focus. Daily
studies are conducted throughout the nation, including medical research centers at the University of Mississippi, University of California at Los Angeles, and the University of Southern California. The
reports are gloomy.

Annihilation of Already Damaged Self Esteem

Intended to elevate one's sense of well-being, long-term use of marijuana appears to be deadly. In time, it destroys the human spirit, the
will to be and do, disolves creative effort, melts away goals, interferes
with sexual functioning, and diminishes capacity for love relationships. Reliance on marijuana and alcohol prevents the individual

from learning to cope with anxiety, tension and self esteem.

The person who distorts reality in consistent measures with any kind of anesthetic faces a dismal future. Indeed, unknown to that self, the present is already dismal. Only the distortions make it seem otherwise.

Some long term marijuana users who stop smoking can recuperate and become fully functioning personalities. Many others cannot retrieve their personal losses, either of self or the love relationships they once had. Never again will they function as effective human beings, whether in work, play, learning, creative efforts, or love.

How to Destroy Your Body

The use of marijuana goes far beyond personality destruction; it lays waste to the body. In the last four or five years, due to special breeding of the weed, marijuana has become ten times more potent. As a result, its use increases the heartbeat dramatically. Unlike alcohol which disappears from the body in hours, three days after a single joint half the marijuana chemicals remain in the body. And days beyond that, many of the chemicals are still deposited in the sexual organs and other systems of the body. There's reason to believe that this residue remains, building up over the years. Destructive effects await the long term smoker.

We now know that a single joint holds as much cancer producing agent as an entire pack of cigarettes. Even more discouraging, since marijuana smoke is inhaled deeper and longer it becomes even more potent as a cancerous killer.

In a product-centered world, demanding praiseworthy behavior in exchange for love, marijuana seems an easy, quick, temporary solution. Eventually, however, each high, every buzz, fades. The same old self esteem problems are left nakedly apparent.

Self Becomes a Part of the Drug

The way a person feels about self is as much a part of any drug's effect as the drug itself. Someone who ordinarily responds favorably to the THC of marijuana may suddenly, with a single joint, suffer a terrifying trip. Frightend, disorganized, the experience becomes one unlike previous effects of the drug. Highs also vary, as well as the level and quality of the buzz.

The condition of the individual's defenses against rage toward loved ones, as well as against self, apparently have much to do with reactions to the THC. When the ego is unsure, with possibilities of loosening the rage which is repressed from awareness, marijuana can be especially frightening in its effects. As in the case of alcohol, what happens when inhaling THC is strongly influenced by the individual's feelings.

More Than Laws are Needed

However physically safe a drug may be, America, indeed societies around the world, is not ready for it. A society that continues to use primitive methods of right and wrong, good and bad to control people, breeds tremendous amounts of anxiety-provoking resentment. As long as this continues, people will insist on drugs to reduce the pain of anxiety about possibly hurting those who make them enraged.

Had marijuana turned out to be what it seemed in the beginning—a drug that, unlike alcohol, didn't destroy the liver, other organs, and the personality — marijuana would still have been, in the interest of humankind, a prohibitive agent. People hurt too much. By far, too many hurt too deeply to be able to ingest any drug that softens or changes reality. Habit dependency, if not addictions, take over the vast majority who use these drugs. When the world puts aside moralistic labels as a way of raising its young, society will be ready to handle mind-changing drugs. But then again, when such a time arrives, there may be no demand for these drugs. The drug-makers may finally be put out of business.

When Law Makers Bury Their Heads

Product-centered society buries its head in sand every time it legislates against beer, booze and marijuana without attending fully to why people insist on having these drugs. The need to use anesthetics is symptomatic of a chronic, deep problem in need of attention. As history has demonstrated time and again, legal efforts to outlaw these anesthetics are unrealistic, as long as no changes are made to rid society of its need for them. Ruined lives and wasted resources continue, as Dr. Slovenko reminds us, in spite of laws.[65] When a nation's personal anguish is so massive and deep, the people, young and old, will find ways beyond the law to anesthetize themselves.

The weekly habit of beer, booze and marijuana is an indictment against a nation's ways of raising its children. Buckling under moralistic pressures to be praiseworthy, resentful, anxious children and teenagers become resentful, anxious adults.

Each generation passes to the next its ways of giving strings-attached love. Millions seek refuge in beer, booze and marijuana. Additional multitudes turn to food hoping to reduce the pain of fallen self esteem. They are no less habit dependent than the marijuana smoker.

BECOMING FAT ON PRODUCT-CENTERED LOVE

Why Diets Never Seem to Work

As an infant your first major daily experience with stress centered around eating. When you were hungry you cried and a parent held and fed you. Your tension evaporated. Within hours you were again experiencing stress, needing food to reestablish your pleasure. It was not only pleasure that you were crying for but a signal, a sign that you as an organism were safe. Being full of food began to mean the same thing as safety to you.

Over the months you started to connect being held, touched and smiled at with taking something into your mouth, swallowing and filling your stomach. These acts began to mean not merely freedom from painful stress but safety.

You were unaware that nutrients of the food coursing through the bloodstream, supplying cells and tissues, were reducing your stress. Future attitudes toward taking food into your mouth, swallowing and keeping a full feeling in your stomach would be tied to anything that made you anxious. When you were with Early Mother her touch, affection and support while feeding you bonded you to her. Later, whenever feeling stress of any kind, but particularly while living in tension-filled product-centered relationships, you would want to eat.

Your hunger would be not for the food but a yearning for touch and affection, love free of moralistic approval and rejection. So it is that the fat person — indeed anyone — need not be hungry or may have just eaten a large meal, in order to be driven to consume more food.

Diets when followed eliminate fat. What is NOT removed is the hungry searching for Early Mother, someone who will love you, all of you, whether or not you do things right. As long as you continue to find self esteem or love through doing what is right and good, resentment will continue, a sense of emptiness prevail, and soon your dieting will have been wasted.

The World as a Breast

Emotional nourishment represented by food may become an insatiable requirement. Your day and night search for tender nourishment, your compulsive drive to find chocolate or other sweets to satisfy the need for sweet, loving touch and other signs of endearment, all are done in hope of filling your hollow life and empty existence. You become overweight, fat, maybe even obese. Each pound above your body's slim, healthy weight is a measure of the love you need, free of labels, but don't get.

OBESE RELATIONSHIPS

Obesity affects millions of adults.[66] It starts earlier, however, in childhood. Thirteen of every one hundred elementary school children at some time suffer obesity. The weight of the anxiety gets turned into fat on their bodies, suffering even greater losses of self esteem.

It is not that obese persons have not been loved in childhood. Indeed, usually there's been plenty of love; consequently they're often friendly and, surfacely at least, happy. They camouflage their dependency, a woefully absent sense of autonomy, by attempts at controlling other people with food. They appear as caring, nurturing persons, when in fact they mostly nurture themselves symbolically by becoming preoccupied with food. They talk about it, buy it, prepare it, cook it and feed it to others. Many never "seem to eat that much." Instead, it is quietly, sometimes secretly nibbled away during preparation and cooking, tiny morsels of rewards for themselves. A mouthful of love here, a mouthful of affection there, all to end upon their bodies, along with a continuing sense of emptiness plaguing them.

THE "OVEREATING, ALCOHOL-DRINKING, MARIJUANA-SMOKING" PERSONALITY

Overeating, marijuana smoking and alcohol drinking on any sort of regular basis constitutes a dependency habit that can make serious inroads on effective living and general happiness. When using alcohol it can become either a habit dependency or it can move a step farther into addiction. The overweight, fat, obese person who is critical of those who are hooked on alcohol or marijuana, is no less habit-dependent on sweets and carbohydrates. Fat persons have been so dependent on someone else's deciding whether they're lovable or not, that they've never assumed responsibility for themselves as persons, as men and women in mature relationships.

Fat persons ordinarily have been successful enough in doing the right things and being a "good person," so that ample love has been received, enough to keep them intact. They're not emotionally disabled. Fat people can function on a job, in society, and even in marriage. The closer their relationships become, however, as in marriage, the less success they have. Often a facade of pleasantness, even jolliness, covers over their deeper feelings. Sweets and carbohydrates act like tranquilizers, much as marijuana does, masking rage over deep feelings of dependency and rage over being "good" as a trade for self esteem.

The Computer Inside Each Overweight Person

Overweight, fat and obese people have handed authority over their lives to others. Like computerized robots they've left their programming to people who surround them. Occasionally fat people suffer a sense of not existing. It's as if someone else owns them. The self belongs to others.[67] It's not unusual, therefore, that obese persons have little or no sense of identity, little sense of self. In order to verify their existence, it's typical for some to look into a mirror. Only then can they be certain that they exist.

At every turn, the mother of the person who is later to become fat directs each move of the child, guiding with a strict set of rights and wrongs, goods and bads. Not always but nearly so, this manipulation is carried out in ways so subtle that no one is conscious of what is happening.

Little wonder that psychotherapy for the fat person is difficult. The self, which is central in therapy relationships, is so much handed over to the therapist that little is left to work with. As with earlier mothering persons, dependence is transferred to the therapist. There's little willingness to deal with the therapist on an independent basis. Instead, the fat person devours the therapist's words, swallowing every gesture, but digesting none of it. They sit hoping for a magical solution for becoming thin. More deeply, they hope to please the therapist by being good, winning perhaps a morsel of self esteem.

Without a sense of being an autonomous self, the individual feels helpless, unable to resist opening the refrigerator to eat. At the moment of going for food, control is elsewhere, in a distant mother or therapist. Emotional supplies of food in the kitchen or candy at the supermarket cannot be resisted. This picture is essentially like that of the alcoholic. Obese persons and regular consumers of marijuana and alcohol live in adult bodies, though like the immature child they demand immediate, quick satisfaction whatever the cost.

Wiring the Obese Person

Obese persons find mothering wherever they can, in a teacher, employer, husband, wife or friend. Since they look to others for control, it's not surprising that some respond to their physicians as a mother, insisting that they be wired with diets, weekly weigh-ins and parental admonitions.

In some cases a physician may actually wire the fat person's jaw closed, making eating impossible. Some lose as many as 55 pounds in six months.[68] Only the "right" kind of eating behavior is possible. Here, control is fully outside the individual, in the physician's wires.

Some fat people assign control outside themselves on a more permanent basis. They have a physician surgically remove part of the digestive system. It is the surgeon, then, who has taken charge. Once again the fat person has remained childlike, passively dependent on authority outside of self.

Overweight Is a Habit Dependency

The center for hunger is actually a place inside your head. Whenever it's stimulated you become hungry. All kinds of chemical-electrical messages inside your body trigger your hunger center when nourishment is necessary. Sometimes, however, need for emotional nourishment — for affection, love and self esteem — is required, and your hunger center gets stimulated even though not physically in need of food. So, feelings can turn on your hunger center just as they can turn off your appetite even when in need of food.

Since fatness is a habit-dependency rather than an addiction, it's easier to treat than when afflicted by drugs. While treatable, fatness resists treatment, as I've already noted, and one would do better to get off the eternal diets and get at the heart of the matter.

I use the word "heart" purposely, because love, the need for affection and self esteem free of right and wrong restrictions, is the very core of the overweight person's need to eat.

In cutting away from dependency on others for feeling positive about oneself, you will have removed the problem. Fatness, overweight of any amount, is a symptom; the problem can be found in product-centered loving. As surely as your product-centered relationships melt away, so also will your excess fat.

THE COMMON THREAD AMONG SICK AND WELL

Certain personality characteristics have been found, in some studies, to be connected with particular physical diseases.[69] Some of these personal traits aren't limited to a single sickness but can be found in a variety of illnesses. The one most frequently found that tends to be a part of most disorders that radically affect cells, tissues and organs of the body, is RESENTMENT. Not resentment in general but specifically toward someone dearly loved.

The loved one who, in these cases, is resented is one requiring right answers, right thoughts, right feelings and right behavior as a down payment on love.

Not only does product-centered love play a critical role in most illnesses, it gets in the way of healthy persons reaching their full potential. By limiting themselves to expectations of others, they're less creative, generally unhappy and not as productive as they would like. Little wonder that resentment takes hold of their life

BURIED RESENTMENT CAN CHANGE YOUR BODY

Most people recognize that feelings have an enormous influence on physical health. To some extent, at least, they accept the role played by emotional tension in heart attacks and headaches. Increasingly, they're becoming aware that feelings can trigger allergies, bronchitis and asthma.

Massive resistance continues, however, in granting that emotions are instrumental in producing changes in tissues and cells (as in cancer), bone disease, tuberculosis, infertility, backache, skin problems, hemorrhoids, teeth-grinding, dental problems, and a host of other disabilities.

Our speech often gives away the close connection between our feelings and body:

I can't stomach him.
He has no guts.
He's gutless.
He makes me sick to my stomach.
It's a gutsy question.
He choked on the question.
When the chips were down he choked.
I can't swallow what you're saying.
It gave me a lump in my throat.
He's a pain in the ass.
My heart jumped.
What a sight for sore eyes.

UNDERNEATH THE SWEETNESS,

A BITTER RELATIONSHIP

There's a strong likelihood that some time in your life you'll be close to someone who will be destroyed by diabetes. Some 10 million Americans are affected in some way by this disease. Every year an estimated 300,000 die of it, either directly or as a result of its complications. It's the fifth leading killer among all diseases.[70] It has been recognized for a long time that your pituitary and adrenal glands have a large role in diabetes. As recently as 1977, San Diego's Scripps Clinic and Research Foundation also cited the important role of the pituitary gland in diabetes.[71] Though specific connections are still being studied, evidence tells us that certain kinds of persons seem more susceptible to diabetes. At any rate, controlling diabetes and staying alive with it are closely connected with human relationships and feelings generated out of them.

Feelings by the Ounce

Physician Flanders Dunbar,[72] in her classic book on psychosomatic medicine, reported that emotions can be measured, literally, in ounces of sugar. One doctor, she wrote, found that a diabetic patient's sugar level increased alarmingly without a change in diet. The patient could be fed certain information which tripped sugar production into action. Ideas, the thoughts of the patient, stimulated measurable increases in sugar.

When Sweet Love Ends in Bitter Resentment

Certain common characteristics and family histories tend to be found in diabetics. Most suffer severe conflict between loving and resenting their parents. Dr. Dunbar found, for example, that most diabetics receive ample affection but from a mother who dominates them, often using conditional love. This combination ends in a resentment relationship with bitter-sweet ingredients.

The harder a diabetic strives to please, producing one expected product after another, the deeper the resentment grows. Later in life distrust of anyone's love, particularly a marriage partner's, leads to a life fraught with unhappiness.

To Each, A Special Way
of Expressing Resentment

Why some turn resentment against the pancreas, others toward their heart, lungs or other organs, is far from being known for sure. It is confident, however, that if resentment isn't dealt with openly, outwardly, it will have its day in attacking the body. Compromises may forestall the reckoning, as in the case of an artist or athlete who redirects wrath into socially acceptable channels.

Such compromises may not be enough. Periodic bouts with alcohol, marijuana, chronic illnesses and sieges of depression may be the symptoms of repressed rage born of unexpressed resentment. For some, as with Ernest Hemingway, art, hunting, fishing and the bull ring no longer work. Rage toward others gets turned against self in a final act of suicide.[73]

ACCIDENTAL RELATIONSHIPS

Feelings of resentful, angry people are revealed in all kinds of ways. More than you ever dreamed possible, the "accident" is often an unconscious loosening of rage. In fact, more often than not the accident is likely not an accident at all. It's anger turned against others or, more often, toward self. Dr. Dunbar has reported that among the millions of major accidents of all kinds taking place yearly, at least 80 percent are unconsciously arranged on purpose.[74] Unable to directly, with a full sense of awareness, strike out against people, they "accidentally" hurt, damage or destroy. When guilt over these feelings of resentment is excessive, instead of accidentally damaging other people, they may "accidentally" hurt themselves.

Dr. Dunbar has also said that accident prone people are frequently found to have had a strict upbringing. As a result they resent people with authority, including parents, teachers, professors, employers, police officers, church, government and, as well, husbands and wives.

In one study, 80 of every 100 persons hospitalized because of an accident were found to be accident prone.[75] As in other studies, the main characteristic of these accident victims was buried resentment turned against themselves.

105

A CRY FOR HELP

The person with bronchial asthma has many characteristics that can contribute to becoming asthmatic. For one thing most find it difficult to cry.[76] A majority of those who do cry, in my own observations, are unable to produce tears. Usually they are unaware that their crying is dry, not tearful.

Dr. Alexander[77] has pointed out that crying is the infant's first way of calling mother. Later, the child becomes afraid to call, fearful of being rejected. Usually the rejection is subtle, hardly detectable by outsiders and, least of all, the mother herself. The mother, Dr. Alexander has said, is "simultaneously seductive and rejecting." She offers her love but only for certain behavior which demonstrates that the infant or child deserves to be valued and loved.

The asthmatic person usually comes from what's often called the "good" home, with high standards and expectations. This is part of the problem. So much energy is spent by the asthmatic trying to do and say things the right way, and being good, that there's little left for spontaneous living and breathing. Each thought, every feeling, all acts, every breath must be self-consciously, cautiously measured and censored before giving them expression.

More than anything else, buried resentment is the asthmatics' characteristic attitude toward one or more persons they deeply depend on and love. Dominated, controlled and manipulated in subtle, undetectable ways, they become angry. At the same time, however, they've learned to feel frightened of their anger, guilty about such feelings.

Fearful of their resentment, asthmatics repress these sorts of angry emotions. When the lid falls on their rage, it also leaves most other feelings trapped deep inside. They no longer have easy, spontaneous access to laughter, sudden erotic expressions or feelings of any kind. Instead they keep themselves busy producing praiseworthy products. Their "good behavior" proves to themselves that they aren't enraged at all, have no destructive feelings toward others, and so should be worthy of being loved and protected.

In my own work with asthmatics, I've found them to be almost always of above average intelligence, frequently superior, although during elementary school years they achieve at average levels.

Anxiety About Resentment Reduces Concentration

Why this discrepancy between the asthmatic's high level intelligence and the ability to learn? It is, I'm certain, anxiety about hidden resentment that interferes with ability to concentrate on what's to be learned. Furthermore, in not learning at high levels, the asthmatic exercises control, if only in a minor way, over one's own life. In this one area, at least, parents and teachers do not get their own way.

The Manipulators Fear Their Own Rage

Those who manipulate the asthmatic are also persons who hold back feelings, especially rage. Their tight controls are often evident in rigid muscular tension, although on the surface they may appear calm and relaxed. Sometimes this tight, rigid posture toward life is communicated to infants only several weeks old. When, for example, a mother bear in the forest communicates danger to her cubs, they freeze up, tighten their muscles and ready their internal body systems to take flight. So it is possible, out of some primitive remnant of human history, that the mother communicates danger to her infant.

However much asthmatics live among tense, tightly controlling people, when they discover that they are free of the "rights and the wrongs," the "goods and the bads," and are lovable for ALL of who they are — every feeling and thought — chances of breathing more easily about themselves approaches 100 percent.

RIGID ARTHRITIC RELATIONSHIPS

Rigid expectations for good behavior are also found frequently in histories of adults with rheumatoid arthritis. They live inside a tightly laced personality, drawing carefully away from life. Fearful of open, spontaneous feelings they become cautious, developing only superficial relationships with loved ones.

Living confined to an emotional straightjacket, they're rigidly, arthritically unable to warmly and flexibly relate to the world. A hard, cold wall separates them from others.

Many arthritics unload their resentment onto substitute persons. While the target of their hidden rage may be someone in the distant past, such as a parent, it may be directed at someone they feel safe with. Victims of their resentment may be a wife, husband or child. When such a victim refuses to any longer be dominated, the arthritic's condition worsens. In rigid, symbolic ways, the physiology of the person with arthritis changes, turning the attack inward on self. Using a homemade form of bio-feedback, muscles and joints tighten, assuming a painfully rigid posture toward their feelings and the people they try to love.

While these observations don't fit all arthritic persons by any means, they can be found with a frequency that must be reported. We're left with an urgency to rid ourselves of right and good, wrong and bad labels used in relating with each other. Doing this we can hope for a more effective society, live a freer, more spontaneous life for ourselves and, in the process, finally realize the lofty goals which today's institutions have subscribed to for so long.

ACID MOUTH RELATIONSHIPS

Your mouth, which was your first connection with getting life-sustaining nourishment, is a center for expressing love and hate. Consequently it's vulnerable to how you feel about yourself. Words from others who manipulate you fall like acid on the picture you have of yourself. One physician said that buried anger can literally change the chemical makeup of your saliva, producing excessive acid in your mouth. In other words certain kinds of things said to you can give you an acid mouth. The part these words play "in creating susceptibility to dental carries is highly influential, if not measurable," says physician Dr. Flanders Dunbar.[78]

Living in a relationship that smolders in resentment not only gnaws at your feelings but eats away at your body. For now, we can only guess at the serious results of product-centered living on dental carries, tooth grinding, softening gums and loss of tooth fillings.

ULCERATED RELATIONSHIPS

If you strongly depend on someone to praise you in order to feel valued, chances are your relationship with that person has a potential ulcer in it. Your ulcerated feelings may begin to attack your body. Sore at a loved one, resentful and wanting to attack with words, an ulcer may appear inside your mouth as a mouth sore.

Or your ulcerated relationship with a parent, husband, wife or other loved one may become deeply buried in the lining of your stomach or intestine. Your digestive system, upset and growling at others, churns out acid that eats away at you. Unable to stomach the way you are required to earn love, aching to be valued for the total impact of yourself, free of right and wrong labels, you experience the pain of an ulcerated life.

Men and women today are equally afflicted with ulcers. This hasn't always been the case. Cultures change their expectations of females and males from time to time, shifting demands for achievement among the sexes.

Core of the Ulcer

Victims of ulcerated relationships have a variety of personality traits. Among these is the person torn between wanting to be dependent on parents, husband or wife and, at the same time, resenting this dependency.

Ulcerated persons, unlike what many people think, aren't go-getters. What seems to be aggressive, go-getter behavior masks anxiety about being submissive. This is unlike the coronary attack victim who strives mightily to be the best, hoping to win love with high achievement products or other socially superior output.

Deep-Seated Ulcerated Relationships

The stronger your mind buries feelings, the more distant these emotions are sent away from your brain and expressed as physical disorders.[79] Persons with stomach disorders, for example, have somewhat different personalities than those with ulcers lower down, in the colon.[80] Wherever an ulcer is located, whatever the type, you can expect to find its core to be resentment.

Most ulcerated persons are so successful at burying their rage that they're thought of by their friends as "really nice persons." These "super nice" individuals bury resentment deeply into the remote regions of their intestines. Here, they express themselves through ulcerative colitis, often weeping blood and diarrhetic discharge through their rectum. A high price is paid for escaping criticism through products of obedience, submissiveness and always sure to be nice.

In the long run, ironically, behavior that's intended to earn them happy, comfortable lives turns out to not work. They suffer pain, become physically ill, and some die earlier than would be necessary.

WHEN YOU CAN'T EXPRESS ANGER
TOWARD PEOPLE OR YOUR BODY

We've seen how people express their anger openly, against others; we've also observed how, unable to spew out feelings, they turn these against the body, become sick, eventually dying. There is yet another way of handling feelings. Some individuals are unsuccessful at expressing anger at others and themselves. Unable to find a target, these persons reduce their painful relationship with life by distorting reality. Their way of looking at themselves and others becomes disordered.

FOUR OF FIVE PERSONS YOU KNOW HAVE MENTAL DISORDERS

A Cornell University team of researchers found that four of five persons in America have serious mental disorders or are painfully neurotic.[81] Furthermore, of every 100 persons, 10 have been, are today, or will be in a mental hospital. Until tranquilizers and other drugs became available, one person somewhere in the United States was admitted every three minutes to a mental hospital for treatment. The same holds true for Canada. This figure alone tells us something about the destructive way in which we raise children and teenagers, and try to change and control each other as adults: through the use of rewards for being right and good, punishments when wrong and bad.

Drugs are intermittent stop-gaps but never solve pain in living with one another. Anxiety about one's self and the tranquilizers and energizers.

Beneath the Masks

Look around you and see energetic people with confident strides and smiling faces. At your office, factory, school and in your community you can hear friendly "good mornings" and "have a nice day." Where are all the sick, unhappy people?

They're all around you, everywhere. They live behind the masks that posture paper-thin smiles. In passing, each looks for evidence that one's self is all right. They search for the slightest human evidence of recognition and affection. One can only guess at the burdens of low self-estimation and empty love carried from homes at the start of each day. Conflict, frustration, depression and lonliness are masqueraded on the surface as happy, contented, fulfilled lives.

For many, the false faces of happiness no longer work for them.

More people are hospitalized with a mental disorder, a Menninger Foundation brochure says, than the combined total of patients with cancer, heart disease, tuberculosis and every other crippling disease. Again it becomes dramatically apparent that the ways we control and relate to one another simply aren't working but spreading havoc upon the societies of the world.

Dr. Ralph Slovenko tells us that, according to the American Schizophrenia Association, 250 Americans a day are diagnosed as schizophrenic.[82] These mentally disordered people not only suffer from daily living but, as Dr. Roderic Gorney points out, die earlier than the general population of the United States. [83]

An Army of Mentally Disordered

Let me make my point again. Everywhere we look there's evidence that our moralistic system of right and wrong — whether it has to do with grading our children and teenagers in school or trying to control their sexual and social behavior — isn't working. It's not even coming close. Worse than not working, the right-wrong, good-bad labeling methods are destroying human happiness and physical health not unlike the plagues that one time swept across Europe.

Here's still another set of massive data that reflects the terrible holocaust visited upon us. During the last World War, 2,564,184 persons were rejected for military service or discharged due to mental disorders. This loss equalled 177 Army Infantry Divisions, or more persons than the total number sent by the Army to the Pacific Theater of war.[84] This same report said that due to mental disorders, one million person-years are lost each year in the work force. Some eight billion dollars a year are lost in earnings by victims of mental disorders, with a billion dollar loss in federal income taxes needed to help run the country.

These figures, like those I reported earlier, illustrate our desperate need to put aside ancient, indeed primitive methods of trying to get people to learn and behave in civilized ways.

Canada, Like the U.S., Also Mentally Disordered

America isn't alone in its chronic epidemic of human misery. The same sort of numbers that reflect American ills also represent Canadians. Numbers are lower, of course, but the percentages are similar.

For example, one in eight Canadians becomes hospitalized with a mental disorder. Emotional suffering disables more Canadian citizens than all other diseases combined. Among the children of Canada, 100,000 become acutely disordered emotionally; 1700 adults commit suicide (15,000 others attempt it); Canadian business and industry lose a billion dollars a year due to mental disorders; one of four adults reduces painful feelings with pills; and 14 of each 100 have the courage to get emotional help from professional workers.[85]

Like Their Parents, Children Suffer Lost Self Esteem

On any given day in the United States, 4,500 children and teenagers are confined in mental hospitals, already suffering critical losses in self esteem and fear of their own resentment[86] Living only 14 years or less on earth, in our homes and schools, they are so disordered that they must be hospitalized. Hundreds of thousands more, while not sent to a hospital, suffer incalcuable misery about themselves, more than anyone should have to bear.

A Mirror Placed Up to Society

The Joint Commission on Mental Illness and Health reported that one of seven persons at some time seeks help for emotional probseeks help for emotional problems.[87] Millions more require professional help but don't search it out. One million Americans live their lives in psychiatric wards each year, with another million getting treatment outside of hospital settings.[88] One of every two hospital beds, in all hospitals across America, has in it a mentally disordered person.[89,90]

Mental anguish is of such epidemic dimensions that an almost impossible tax burden is faced yearly in caring for these people. New York, for example, employs more than 50,000 persons simply to operate its mental health program.[91]

Think of all the police calls reported in every town and city of America day after day, week upon week, the year around. Ninety percent "are from citizens who need help with problems of everyday living or with problems which do not involve violation of criminal statutes."[92]

"We Kill the One We Love the Most"

Most anger, violence and tragedy occur in close, everyday relationships. *Destruction among human beings takes place more often among people who know each other, especially in some kind of intimate relationship,* than it does between strangers.

Indeed, half of all murders occurs during the marriage quarrel. In this intimate relationship one of every two murders takes place.

As an added irony, men kill their women most often in the bedroom, a special place of rest, intimacy and love. Women, on the other hand, murder men most frequently in the kitchen, a special place for gathering together for nurturance and refurbishing. Pain, conflict, disease and destruction, most of it unnecessary, are occuring everywhere around us, born of ancient resentment. It's as if there's some law that says the closer people get to one another, the more dangerous and destructive they become.

What appears to be a "law" is the consistency with which we deny each other a sense of self esteem. In the primitive tradition we continue making ourselves and others feel wrong and bad as persons, particularly so when we resent others' demand that we be right and good as a condition for getting their affection.

Relationships, Not Instincts,
Trigger Your Angry, Aggressive Feelings

Both you and lower animals have a rage center that is inherited equipment. It is a place in your brain with minute, electrical-like hookups. When stimulated it prods one to attack.

In the case of animals, their rage center goes into action only when stimulated by physical attack or threat of losing food, babies or sexual mates. It works automatically and is said to operate by instinct.

Contrary to common opinion, animals attack only in the above, very special conditions. They prefer to run away rather than fight. Only humankind, with its higher, more developed brain centers makes war on one another, slaughtering its own kind as individuals or enmassed as groups called nations.

War-like as humans can become, they prefer, like animals, to safely withdraw in the face of either physical threat or danger to self esteem. Angered by threats to their self-estimation, but with nowhere to run —as is so often the case in complex human relationships—they withdraw psychologically. Rage is concealed from others and, using a uniquely developed ability among humankind, becomes hidden even from themselves. These furious feelings are repressed, but only for the time being. They must have their day. When unable to get spent outwardly, onto others, their fury spends itself on one's own body. Sickness follows.

Disguising Your Attacks on Others

Most of your urges to hit out at someone have nothing to do with physical danger. Hostile, aggressive wishes toward others are almost always the outcome of their threatening your self esteem. When they lower your self estimation this automatically triggers your rage center into action.

Unlike animals who are physically endangered in some way and make a simple reaction to it, you act out of complicated meanings. More than things themselves, you react to symbols. Certain behaviors, objects or events symbolize something to you — something that may not actually be present.

Just as subtly, and often in hidden or disguised ways, you strike out at those who, as you understand it, are lowering your self esteem or make you feel less lovable. Direct, open, frontal attacks on others aren't ordinarily used by you. Concealing your wrath you protect yourself from further rejection, real or imagined. When it seems too risky to attack in even disguised ways, you hold back your anger and, as it builds and smolders, you turn it against your own body. This, unconsciously of course, seems safer than hitting out at those you love. Some part of your body gets sick.

Disguising Anger With Being Nice

Some persons, unable to get out their resentment, become "nice," quiet, "good" persons who consistently please everyone. They aren't noble at all, however, but only defensively protecting their self esteem. Being nice and good they put themselves beyond criticism, playing it safe. The price for this is high.

They sacrifice their spontaneity and great bursts of creative energy, suffering a sense of lost autonomy. "Right" and "wrong," "good" and "bad" control what they feel, think and what they do. They follow these superficial stars, whose light burned out centuries ago, thinking that they'll be led into more satisfying work, play, human relationships and sexual expression.

PART FIVE

TAKING
RIGHT AND WRONG
GOOD AND BAD
OUT OF SEX

EXPLORING YOUR GENITALS

As a child you soon learned that having pleasure in different parts of your body alarmed people. You found, for example, that sucking your thumb, pleasurable as it was, upset them. They told you that it would ruin your teeth. Somehow, though, you sensed that their concern was more an embarrassment than anything. Their revulsion made you feel ashamed, guilty and bad.

When you touched your genitals they pulled your hand away. You momentarily lost self esteem. Their efforts to be subtle didn't fool you; you got the idea and withdrew from your natural, spontaneous curiosity and pleasure. "If it's so important for them to hide the fact that they're distracting me, then I'll hide it from myself." Most of us don't remember their efforts to turn us away, in shame, from our genitals. These experiences live on, however, in the deep regions of our unconscious, continuing to influence personal and sexual behaviors. All this was but one more surrender of spontaneity. You were on your way to losing touch with yourself and others.

They Spell Freud S-E-X

Today's attitudes toward sex have relaxed somewhat, becoming more realistic and suffering fewer taboos. The pioneering efforts of Sigmund Freud must be credited for much of this hard won freedom. Yet no one is more villianized. Criticisms spent on him on any single day in America must exceed that of any other individual, living or dead. And it continues, very much alive, one generation after another.

If Freud Has Been Dead 40 Years, Why's He Still Alive?

Year after year you'll find that, along with Shakespeare, the author of the most books at popular bookstores is Freud. His name appears more often in books and magazines, human behavior journals, television and movies, than any other person living or dead. Why, then, is he so rejected?

Sex and Freud have come to mean the same thing. Having been taught to reject sexual wishes, people find Freud's ideas threatening. Often those who shout loudest against him have read him least. Others, those who've read bits and pieces of what he wrote, or have merely listened to what others have said, concentrate on his errors, denouncing his place in history.

Freud's Miscalculations

Some of Freud's horrendous miscalculations and biased views went uncorrected by him. Yet more than anyone, then or since, he modified, changed and retracted his theories throughout his long life. It was common for him to withdraw earlier ideas, and advance new ones in their place, making new discoveries to the end.

Freud's ability to say "I was incorrect," then move forward, goes unmatched by anyone. His history shows, for example, were he living today no one would be more embarrassed at his writings on women than himself. Just as he introduced the common use of cocaine to the world for dental and everyday tension-reduction purposes, only with guilt to later announce its potential hazards, so could we expect his errors in understanding women. Indeed, had Freud lived into the 1940's and 1950's his growing insight might have led the way to an earlier women's liberation movement.

Freud's influence in history is everywhere in our daily lives. Still, the sound of his name continues to irritate in ways that say sex is still denied us as a natural condition in our human rights.

THE GREAT COVERUP

Modesty Not a Matter of
Clothes or No Clothes

The first MAJOR breakthrough putting sex on a scientific basis came with the genius and courage of Havelock Ellis.[93] His work began the difficult journey of removing sex from a purely speculative, emotional and religious basis.

While Ellis' work is more than 70 years old, much of his report represents history that in many ways remains useful today. It provides a backdrop against which ignorance, myths and superstition stand out as reminders to us to be wary of distortions made of sex today. Further, Ellis' efforts were necessary, early steps toward giant strides taken by Kinsey, Pomeroy, Martin, and Gebbard,[94,95] Masters and Johnson, [96] and others marching toward freedom from indentureship to fearful, guilty attitudes about sex.

Havelock Ellis' history of early peoples who were unspoiled by product-centered civilization abounds with evidence that modesty has nothing to do with clothing. People were modest long before clothing was invented.

Modesty is psychological. It occurs when eyes are drawn to an individual in a particular way not necessarily related to sex. It leaves the person with a kind of self-consciousness that can be felt whether clothed or not. A person or an entire culture must be taught to feel immodest without clothes.

Naked Modesty and Integrity

We assume that clothes became popular out of a practical need to keep warm, shield the body from insects and bush, or to protect one from sexual molestations. Studies of primitive tribes don't support this. Many tribes before the arrival of white people simply didn't wear clothes at all. In Central Australia, for example, clothes weren't worn even when the climate was uncomfortably cold.

Although living in nakedness, these people's behavior, by present-day standards, reflected the highest possible integrity. In fact, historical evidence shows that in matters of sexual conduct they surpassed, by far, today's clothed society.

It's true, of course, that in severe climates, as migrations of earliest people moved northward and polar icecaps edged south, clothes were worn for warmth. But in climates where this was not the case clothes were introduced for other reasons.

Central Australians, cited above, wore decorations as attention-getters rather than coverups, such as decorative headgear and armbands. At times women wore only a decorative, suggestion-sized cloth over their genitals. They were lax or unconcerned whether the cloth covered them at all. Men at times wore a brilliantly colored tassel tied around their penis, especially at social events.

As late as the 1500's nakedness was common in Germany. No one, for example, wore clothing to bed or at the public bath. Throughout the Middle Ages, in fact, women wore no underclothes. English women thought panties to be immodest and unfeminine. Prostitutes were the first to wear panties, having gotten the idea probably from the Orient. They were certain that in covering their genitals with panties men would be all the more seduced. In other words, panties were introduced more to create sexual interest and excitement than to ward them off. It was only later, on the advice of physicians, that panties began to be worn as a hygienic measure.

Two Inches of Modesty

Ellis also pointed out artist Du Maurier's comment, "nothing is so chaste as nudity," and Burton's observation that clothes are the greatest provocations of lust. The entire history of clothing, like it or not, seems to support modern advocates of designated nude beaches.

Such beaches disturb much of the public today, but keep in mind that as recently as the 1920's women were being sent to jail because they sat on beaches in bathing suits without sleeves or stockings.

Ellis reports that on September 26, 1898, England's daily papers decreed that women should be two inches more modest than men. Women's bathing suits were to be two inches longer than men's at both the knee and arm. In this same year, in Philadelphia, the *Ladies Home Journal* decided never to mention women's undergarments. The term "unmentionables" was coined, in order to never offend women's modesty. Only today, slowly, is the behavior product of modesty being equalized between men and women.

WOMEN AS PROPERTY

It has been said that clothes got a boost in importance when men began to view women as property. Ellis wrote that Schurtz and Letourneau, and later Diderat in the eighteenth century, insisted that jealousy of husbands was the main reason clothing was worn. In some cultures married women wore clothing, but not men nor single (unowned) women. It was product-centered values, not modesty, that introduced the idea of clothing.

Women today are beginning to become aware that personal appearance is a matter of their own choice. No longer is it necessary that a woman invitingly redden her lips, wear dresses instead of slacks, or in other ways produce products traditionally expected of them by society in general and men in particular. Women can, if they give themselves their own permission, buy into whichever products they choose without social prescriptions dictating every decision about how they want to live their womaness.

Much of this freedom has emerged as women feel less owned by their so-called protective parents, men. New options include opportunities to earn their own living, enter more and more professions, and make decisions about whether or not to have children.

TAKING YOUR UTERUS OFF THE MARKET

Never before has it been so possible for women to experience a sense of worth based on the total impact they have on their world, without having to feel right or wrong, good or bad. Most haven't capitalized on this opportunity, but the time is ripe. Risky as it may seem, living life according to what is effective for you—what works—rather than being guided by trying to be right and good to please others, is more available than ever before.

The uterus is a distinguishing characteristic of the female. She need not use this any longer, however, to establish her worth as a person. Her value, her lovableness, need not be set by her vagina and uterus. The time has come, after centuries of being otherwise, for women to value themselves by other than sexual functions.

Entertaining men, affording them pleasure (often while denying their own) and giving them babies need no longer be the benchmark of a woman's desirability. Moreover it's time — past time — for her own feelings, thoughts, wishes, conflicts, hopes, goals, dreams, fears, joys, anxieties, guilt, and physical requirements to be given full recognition. She need but make it so, presenting herself to herself and others as someone who is inseparably a woman-person-female. In doing this you, as a woman, break free of presenting your femaleness as a product separate from yourself.

In ancient Egypt the woman's reproductive function was of such immense importance that men devised ways to determine when women could conceive a child.[97] Garlic was placed in the vagina, and when it was detectable on the woman's breath within 12 hours, this indicated that she was fertile. Still another way used by Egyptians was to have the woman squat over a container of date flower and beer made of barley. If she became nauseated and vomited from smelling the fumes, she was ready to conceive a baby.

Validating Your Worth Through Your Uterus

Obviously, when one's worth is so deeply tied to the uterus, threat to its productivity can be a focus for severe emotional problems. Greeks of early Europe recognized this, though explaining it in mystical ways. Neurotic behavior of women was thought to result from a wandering uterus with "sickening conditions spreading from it," turning them into hysterical creatures.

Thanks to Freud and Breuer we began to know, of course, that the uterus doesn't cause mental disorder, but that unrealistic, fearful attitudes toward it can. Even today, however, attitudes of this kind continue to plague women. Four of 100 women with hysterectomies develop severe depression over their loss. More than most, these women have invested their sense of productivity and value deeply in their uterus. Without it they feel stripped of their worth.

Beneath the False Faces of Love

The little girl who grows into womanhood obligated to be a certain kind of person, separating her sexuality from who she is, offering it as a product in return for self-esteem, quickly becomes resentful. This is also true of males, certainly, but the woman has an added dimension to live by: her reproductive capacity. By far, it dictates her worth in a society that turns sexual functions into products that determine the individual's loveableness.

While males are taught to curb or redirect resentment and anger, the female even more so must hold angry aggression inside her, pretending other feelings on the surface. Frightened of her anger, lest it betray her as a bad person, she denies it not only to others but herself.

Presenting a facade of pleasantness, she believes in her masquerade and acts honestly, as she sees her conscious self to be. In time, however, unless released from demands to be good as a way of winning love, resentment eats at her happiness and body.

In particular, when conflict revolves around how she sees herself as a woman, mother, the organs of her sexual functions may become sick of it all. Cells may begin to run cancerously wild, with tissue changes threatening life itself. Her cervix is destroyed in a rage of disease.

Cooling Desire

What has been the cancer of her feelings becomes the cancer of her body. Often the woman who expresses resentment through her cervix is also one who throws cold water over the heat of her sexual excitement. Motherhood becomes a drag, a nuisance, and all functions related to it.

In one study of women with cancer of the cervix, a significant number had a personality profile like many who develop breast cancer. A chief difference, though, was a greater sexual inhibition in women with cervical cancer.

While it needs to be emphasized, EMPHATICALLY, that not all women who suffer cancer of the cervix have the so-called cervix personality profile, it happens often enough to make us sensitive to the part feelings play in not only happiness but body health.

DON'T LET THEM TEACH YOU THE "MENSTRUAL BLUES"

Sing your own song. Dance life to your own tune. You can, you know. It's unnecessary to live a monthly song of depression. Your "period" can be a breeze; it need not be a raging storm of hormones.

"That's what YOU say. You're a man. How could you know? Get off our backs and let us sing the menstrual blues. Let us have our cramps, irritability, backaches, headaches, skin problems, tender breasts, weight gain, restlessness and crying spells."

Most agree that premenstrual tension is fairly common, but how common no one really knows. There seems to be ample evidence that 70 percent endure this sort of tension.[98] This same report also notes that some who suffer are unaware of it, but others are. Co-workers or friends of these women notice increased irritability and upheaval in personal relationships. Industries hiring women claim that premenstrual tension results in costly errors, accidents and generally ineffective work. Also, premeditated crimes increase during premenstrual tension.[99]

Menstrual Blood Treated as a Product

Throughout the history of humankind menstrual blood has had a profound influence on women — due mostly to men's fear of it. Male attitudes have led women to view themselves as unclean, even dangerous.

Havelock Ellis' classical studies report that at one time Surinam women were isolated during mentruation. They were convinced, men and women alike, that anyone near a menstruating woman was in danger. If persons inadvertently approached her, she would cry out, "I'm unclean!"

When Chiriquano women of Bolivia menstruated, elderly females would, stick in hand, hunt the snake (penis?) that wounded the woman. In Germany, until the eighteenth century, people were convinced that a buried hair from a menstruating woman would become a snake.

In South America, menstruating women were suspended in a hammock near the roof, "between heaven and earth," as they say, so that "dangerous influences" wouldn't harm anyone. In New Zealand she was elevated above ground level in a dark, narrow cage. In other parts of the world, as with the Arapesh in New Guinea, she spent her period in isolated huts, away from people.

Evil, Mythical Powers of Menstruating Women

Still other "bad" labels have been fastened onto women through their sexually related behavior products. Early in this century people of northern France kept menstruating women out of sugar refineries, so that during boiling and cooling periods the sugar wouldn't turn black. In 1878, the *British Medical Journal* reported that meat would spoil if cured by a woman having her period. Menstruating women have been said to sour milk, spoil wine and possess other destructive powers. They were accused of making violin strings break, needles snap and clocks stop. (This reminds one of modern superstitions which hold that some persons have mental powers to bend keys, stop clocks and float bodies in the air.)

Today's Menstrual Myths

Studies reported by psychologist Dr. Karen Paige tell us that menstrual mythologies continue to plague women.[100] Fluctuating hormone levels, Dr. Paige reminds us, occur in all women, but not all react with tension, irritability, weight increases, cramps and other pains. Researcher Paige also noted that women's attitudes about themselves, their bodies and men they live with also vary remarkably.

In one survey, for example, it was reported that half the men and women had never experienced sex during menstruation. It was thought of as dirty or frightening and, in many cases, forbidden by higher authority.

Dr. Paige also studied women whose hormone levels were kept fairly constant by using the pill. Any differences in women's symptoms, therefore, couldn't be attributed to a rage of hormonal changes before and during their period. For the most part she found that:

1. Women on the pill who had less bleeding than before reported fewer symptoms. They also had less anxiety.

2. Women on the pill whose bleeding remained normally heavy continued to have their usual menstrual symptoms and anxiety.

3. Women on and off the pill whose flow was normally heavy had the same menstrual symptoms and anxiety.

Society has convinced many women that menstrual blood is a sign of being unclean and inferior. Some interpret it, unconsciously, as a surgical loss of a penis, which is a reminder to men that they could lose theirs, either physically or symbolically and become, therefore, passive, dependent, helpless victims roaming the earth.

Women who count on their sexuality to give them self esteem will inevitably think less of themselves during their period. Feeling less valued they become anxious, resentful and are plagued with one sort of symptom or another. Little wonder that they become irritable and cramped.

On explorer Perry's expedition to Greenland, Ellis tells us, his ethnologist discovered that menstruation didn't start among women until they were 19. Moreover, only 10 percent of menstruating women did so during the long winter months when people moved together in close protection against the brutal cold.

On the Faroe Islands menstruation was reported to be almost totally absent. Certain tribes of North American Indian women had only scanty periods, while full-blooded Crow Indians menstruated in ways similar to white women.

Women of all races and cultures have the same kind of physiology and child bearing functions. Yet menstruation differs widely. It's reasonable that cultural values, expectations, feelings and self-pictures are a part of every woman's period. Those who refuse to think of menstruation as a sign of unworthiness suffer less distress or none at all.

They need not join the national chorus that sings the menstrual blues.

If Not Hormones, What Then?

To begin with, women with less flow are less troubled with simply taking care of it. Further, twice as many of these women have sex during their periods. This reduces tension and lets them live as if there's nothing wrong with them.

Religious attitudes also play a significant role in the aches and pains of women. Dr. Paige reminds us that Catholic, Jewish and Protestant women all have the same hormones. Yet they differ in menstrual tension and anxiety.[100]

Orthodox Jewish women are restricted from having sex during their period and the following seven days. They're seen as unclean. They must have a ritual cleansing before sexually approaching a man. Psychologist Paige, recalling Portnoy's complaint, found Jewish women to be "uniformly anxious all month."

It's reported that the Catholic Church stresses that women not have sex while menstruating. Women are an "unclean vessel that tempts the pure man." Dr. Paige's study found Catholic women to have an extreme rise in anxiety prior to menstruating.

Protestants have a wide variety of denominational attitudes toward having sex during a woman's period. With no strong restriction against it, Protestant women showed very little change in anxiety between midcycle and the time just before onset. Twice as many Protestant women have sex during menstruation as Catholic and Jewish women. The influence of attitudes is apparent.

Finally, Dr. Paige found that women who suffer menstrual problems are also prone to all kinds of symptoms throughout the month. They use more pills and have more aches and pains not related to their period.

Personal Safety Can Affect Menstrual Flow

In Nazi Germany's death camps Jewish women were not only devalued as unclean potential menstruaters, but also as persons doomed to be extinguished for being Jewish. Their very lives were moment-to-moment events, with little assurance that they would exist in the next hour. With constant threats and dehumanizing treatment, they stopped menstruating and didn't resume until liberated.[101] Perhaps no more convincing evidence than this can be found to dramatize the influence that thoughts and feelings can have on menstrual behavior, aches, pains, cramps and other ways of reacting to your period.

BABY PRODUCTS

Buried resentment can change the supply of blood to your head, giving you a headache. The same holds true for the fallopian tubes. They can "tighten up," so to speak, when feeling anxiety about self, fear of childbirth, uncertainty about being an adequate mother, and anger toward men who are unconsciously seen as powerful, destructive and dangerous to one's personal autonomy. Sperm are shut out. Pregnancy, for the time at least, becomes impossible.

Feelings Can Make Slow Swimmers of Sperm

A similar process holds true for men. Physicians have noticed that a man's anxiety about self can prevent fertilization of the ovum.[102] Sperm count is not a fully adequate measure of whether a male is potent. Levels of the sperm's quality and activity are what count. Although illness and fatigue can be influential, physician Dr. Flanders Dunbar said that these make little difference as long as a man is free of anxiety. Conflict about himself, women, his sexual behavior as a product to be graded from "A" to "F," are instrumental in being unable to fertilize a woman. Having to be the right kind of sexual partner, a good person, triggers sufficient resentment to change his physiology. His sperm, in some cases, are simply no longer able to swim strongly and certainly to their goal, penetrate the woman's ovum, and thereby be a part of creating another human being.

BUYING SELF ESTEEM
WITH YOUR BREASTS

We live in an age of breast fixation. Breasts have become products of immense significance. Few women and fewer men have successfully escaped the fetish.

Is it because breasts extend from the body, differentiating her femaleness from males? The more they extend, the more female she is? Or is it that they represent, if only symbolically, the original nurturing Early Mother? Could it be that the larger the breasts the more they signal a promise of unconditional infant love? Whatever the answer, big breast products are buying self esteem for women in the male marketplace.

Small Breasts as Desirable

From time to time cultures change their attitudes toward breasts. In some regions of early Europe, for example, men thought that large breasts were disgusting. During the female's breast development years she forcefully tied flat stones to her chest, hopefully discouraging growth. She knew that small breasts, tiny like daisies, turned men on; chrysanthemum-sized ones turned them away. Like women of today, they took their cues for gaining or losing self esteem according to the sexual products they possessed.

Another View of Breasts

It has been written that in 1600 Naga women of Assam covered only their breasts. They thought it ridiculous to cover genitals, since individuals were born with these. Breasts came later and so should be covered.[103] Naga people would be as shocked at our exposure of breasts as we would at their nonchalant exposure of genital organs.

Taking Charge of Your Own Breasts

When you depend on your breasts as a source of gaining or losing self esteem, you become separated from them. Your breasts become objects not only to men but to yourself, attachments owned and used but not integrated as a part of your person.

When you are believed to be valued for your breasts rather than the total impact of your person, resentment starts to grow. Your relationships with yourself and men begin to suffer, although this happens mostly in your unconscious self and, therefore, you're unaware of it. Nevertheless it has a powerful influence on you. Resentment, growing into anger, eventually becomes deeply buried rage.

In one way or another, as long as you try to get self esteem by producing "good" sexual products, your resentment will eat away your intimate relationships. You'll find yourself, over the years, moving in and out of relationships or remaining miserably inside the one you have, too fearful to move.

Making Your Own Breast Choices

You can decide to have your breasts enlarged, made smaller, or lifted for reasons other than having to fit someone else's expectations as a price for collecting self esteem. You can do so, if you choose, out of the impact these changes have on you in experiencing your own body. You can enjoy whatever pleasantness or excitement that alterations in your body lines give you in relationships with both yourself and others.

This differs from making breast choices as a way of making yourself feel lovable. Obviously, of course, breasts can have the effect of drawing people to you, but lovableness comes out of your person — from the total impact of who you are. In other words, feelings about your womanness can be yours without the destructive limits of having to look like the "right" sort of person. Self esteem of this kind, unlike that obtained for being "good," is more enduring. It frees you from resentment.

Trapped by Your Need to Feel Independent

It's common for people in search of personal autonomy to trap themselves inside their need to resist. In order to prove to the world and themselves that they're independent, they resist doing what they would really enjoy. They prefer the pleasure of resisting someone's control.

Some women, for example, who wish to make surgical changes in their breasts, may deny themselves this to prove to the world (and themselves) that "you must accept me as I am; I will not be pressured into having the kind of breasts that society says are attractive."

These women are no more free than the one who spends time presenting her body as a major way of feeling self-worth. They're imprisoned by a need to prove something. While deep down, out of their own pleasure it would afford, they may want to surgically enlarge or uplift their breasts, they defensively resist.

The impact woman can change her appearance if she chooses without feeling dishonest. She doesn't feel that she's presenting a false front to the world, nor selling out her integrity in payment for praise.

IN THE BEGINNING THERE WAS A CLITORIS, AND THEN, BEHOLD, THERE WAS A PENIS

clitoris . . . : a small organ at the anterior
or ventral part of the vulva
homologus to the penis

penis . . . : a male organ of copulation

(Excerpted from Webster's New Collegiate Dictionary (c) 1979 by G. & C. Merriam Company, publishers of the Merriam-Webster Dictionaries.)

Penis Envy: What Women"Really" Want

Earlier than you would guess, the little girl discovers that males are given more rights. Boys can get dirty, swear, fight, climb trees and wander farther from home. Reprimands for any of these acts are not as severe or serious as with girls. It seems to the girl, therefore, that boys enjoy more tolerance and freedom, have greater power over their own lives.

"How are boys different from me?" she asks. The only obvious difference is a penis. Consequently it becomes a symbol not only of maleness but freedom, authority and power. In a world that values authority and power, the penis, as their representative, comes to be valued. It's easy to understand why folklore and theories explaining human behavior talk about *penis envy*.

The penis is "extra." It's something more than no penis. Living in a product-centered world, where most people earn daily rations of self esteem with producing good products — and often, MORE of anything is thought to be better and good—the girl may, if only in her unconscious self, wish that she owned a penis. This product could, she assumes, bring her more autonomy, a sense of greater freedom and self-worth.

Penis Handicap

It could be that the penis is a handicap. One writer, Anne Ardent, wrote a book called *Penis Pity*. She may be accurate! Doesn't that funny looking thing hanging down, that appendage, get in the way? you might ask. It has to be tucked in and taken out, washed, circumsized, and, along with the testicles, carefully protected. Moreover, it has to stand up to get its greatest pleasure.

Psychoanalytical theory suggests that women (and men) believe that, in and of itself, to not have a penis is a loss. Women, it's said, feel this loss deeply and it affects them throughout their lifetime. Men, while having a penis, fear that they'll lose it.

Wanting a penis or fearing that, having one, it might be cut off, does not happen out of nothing. It isn't instinctual or inherited. Only in giving the penis — having one or possibly losing it — MEANING, meaning that's socially or culturally invented, can it become an object of envy.

The Penis as a Symbol of Equal Rights

Why is it then that they say women envy a man his penis? Indeed if they do — and clinical evidence supports this — it's not a penis that's wanted. It's equality of power and opportunity. Women want full rights to job access, leadership and life styles. They, themselves, want to choose marriage or not, "sow their wild oats" or not, have babies or not, without being controlled by "shoulds" and "should nots," rights and wrongs, goods and bads. Men make decisions, run governments, send nations off to the slaughter of war, and dominate daily living. The penis becomes the flag for this lop-sided power. If it's a penis women want, then penis is spelled e-q-u-a-l-i-t-y in human rights.

Women want to experience the full impact of who they are. They want to make decisions on the basis of what's *effective* or *ineffective,* what *works* or *doesn't work.* It is intolerable to continue having one's life dominated by desperate efforts to think and say and do what is right and good, in order to feel worthwhile and lovable. Moralistic controls inherited from ancient civilizations are centuries overdue for extinction. They've outlived their usefulness, have become — indeed always have been — destructive to the human spirit and physical well-being.

The irony is that moralistic control negates, defeats in every way, the "moral" civilization that we seek. Beneath the surface of every woman throbs the need to break free of primitive codes which stipulate that to be lovable she must first be right and good. Her subjugation is about to end.

She requires more than the erotic experiences of herself and the one she loves. The relationship must exceed the old moralisms and repressive dictums of right and wrong guiding how each relates to the other. Lucy Freeman in her brilliant book, *What Do Women Want?*, calls for a relationship that has not only passionate, erotic love but one based on "friendship and trust . . . respect and admiration . . . a love that contains in it the wish to share, comfort and help."[104] The essence of such a love is in no longer labeling one's self and the other as right and good, wrong and bad, and instead sharing the IMPACT that each has on the other.

Rather than moralizing as good or bad, each shares the delight, concern, passion, doubts, hopes, fears, erotic needs, helplessness, power, and all the other countless personal experiences which are any human being. All is shared in trust and friendship, respect and admiration, in the need to receive and give comfort and help. The extent that this is possible in any relationship will mostly depend on how much product-centered, right-wrong evaluations are replaced by IMPACT-centered ones.

WHEN THE CLITORIS BECOMES A PENIS

While some men and women are proud of the appendages that distinguish them, these organs aren't that different in origin. This is so because every human embryo begins development as a female and turns into a male only if certain hormones are present. In a sense, therefore, every male, however proud of his penis, started out life not with a penis but a clitoris.

In the case of very young females, when nature goes astray and adds extra androgen to her system, the clitoris begins to grow. As early as age three in these particular girls the clitoris starts to look like a penis, and pubic hair appears. As the girl grows so does her clitoris, until in shape and length it appears to be a penis, sometimes reaching several inches in length. In all respects, except for her penis-like appendage, she is a female.

Myths About Your Clitoris

Just as there are erroneous ideas about the importance of penis size, myths also exist about your clitoris. First, the size of your clitoris has nothing to do with the amount of pleasure you get from your orgasms.

Also, whether your clitoris becomes hard and elongated or remains in its soft form during sex doesn't determine how intensive your orgasms will be. It's possible, however, that your orgasms may diminish if you focus on folklore that measures your womanness by the size of your clitoris during sex. In fact, any time you focus on having to measure up to sexual expectations, trouble is in store for you in your sex life.

Fear of being inadequate and failing to be "good" at it leads to resentment that interferes with sexual functioning. Sex becomes an act, a measurable product, defeating the experience. The relationship goes downhill.

PENIS AS A PRODUCT

Putting Your Penis On A Pedestal

Throughout history most religions (conceived and maintained mostly by men) have given organs of reproduction a special emphasis, often a position of worship. These organs symbolize continuation of life around which religions are built, suggesting power to survive.[105]

According to Hindu religious belief the gods Brahma and Vishnu were created from non-beings.[106] At the same time of their creation, as it turns out, there was a huge, splendid Lingam, or phallus. This penis was so huge that years of deep searching at its base and at the upper stratospheres for its top ended in failure. It is also reported that while Lingayats are puritanical, they "always carry their god-symbol with them—the carved Lingam or phallus."

Not all of society consistently gives your penis such a high place. Where it's revered, it's also attacked. At about the time it's put up for admiration, it's put down as dirty.

WHAT THEY TAUGHT YOU
ABOUT YOUR PENIS

As a male you had your earliest, most critical experiences identified with the soft, tender care of a woman. As a result you'll never lose your need to receive and give soft, tender care throughout your life. Whether or not you're aware of it, your life has been influenced by this need more than anything else.

In spite of your tender needs, society has bred a sense of machoism in you. You must "be a man"; you're required to avoid all appearances of womanness. You're asked to repress your powerful drive to be soft, tender and touching. It's expected that you stand erect and hard, pushing forward in the business world, athletics and socially. To thrust yourself aggressively to the head of society is also to earn your right to self esteem in society's product-centered set of rights and wrongs.

Being a Male Is Different From Being a Man

"Manness" and "maleness" aren't the same thing. Being a man is part of being a person. Being a male, on the other hand, is a biological condition.

How you look at your biological maleness, what you think about it, is part of your identification as a man. Much of your focus as a man, a person, is on your penis. Society has turned your head in this direction. Though simply another biological organ, your penis has taken on an enormous importance, becoming the center of seeing your self as a man and a person.

PENIS STATUS

Conditional Penis Status

You were taught that your penis has only limited, conditional acceptance. Monstrous prohibitions have been put on handling and looking at it. Much of what you learned about it, its function and place in your life, was expressed through myths. You were told that masturbation, for example, will give you pimples, make you go crazy, deplete your athletic performance, or cause blindness.

In early infancy masturbation was discovered by you as a source of pleasure. At times your penis became stimulated, felt pleasurable and stood as an erect testament to the excitement of being alive. After awhile, though, unspoken messages said that this pleasure was forbidden. To do the right thing, be a good person, and preserve your self esteem, you learned to hide your pleasure. In your very earliest years you stopped stimulating yourself, and later, between the ages of nine and fourteen when you returned to self-stimulation, you tried hard— but without success—to "stop playing with yourself."

You were convinced that stimulating your genitals was somehow potentially dangerous, if not physically then certainly in your attempts to have others think well of you. You had to hide your penis from the world, especially the pleasure you got from it, and by all means keep it away from girls. You began to have mixed feelings about your body. Somewhere deep inside, beyond awareness, you began to separate your penis from who you were as a person. In order to stimulate it you had to do so only under darkly hidden circumstances. This protected you from the stamp of evil and lost self esteem.

Later in life, when you unwrapped your penis to make love, you found it difficult to include your self, your person, in love-making. Your person stood to one side, evaluating what your penis was accomplishing, whether it rated an "A" or "C" or "F."

DIMENSIONS OF YOUR PENIS

When you use your penis to validate your self esteem it gets turned into a product alienated from your person. As a result you become self-conscious of it. Your ideas and values begin to interfere with your feelings which, in turn, influence your hormones. In fact your entire physiology changes. Sex drive, erections, orgasms, sexual satisfaction, all are affected in negative ways when you see your penis—what it does—as a product to be judged right or wrong.

In other words, self-judgmental thoughts lessen affection, love and erotic feelings. No matter how much your sex hormones are present, they can't compete with self-judgments about your penis in love-making. You become a candidate for any one of many levels of frigidity or impotence. This may range from inability to get erections or have an orgasm, to being able to have erections and orgasms but not experience the kind of personal, tender, loving relationship that provides the fullest possible personal satisfaction which nourishes love.

The fact that human beings have more layers of higher brain tissue than do animals, in order for a fully functioning sex life to be possible, a personally involved, non-good-bad relationship is inextricably a part of the sex act. Animal sex is limited to a seasonal basis, but humankind, because of higher brain centers, is sexually active all year.[107] It is these higher tissue levels that do, indeed, make how you see yourself — your self esteem and sense of lovableness — a critical part of your sex life.

Penis Size and Other Myths

Do you wonder about the physical dimensions of your penis? "Wondering" about it can't interfere with your sex life, but product-centered concern can. Masters and Johnson have said that while there's great variation in the size of soft penises, this is not so when they become erect.[108] "The smaller penis," they've found, "engorges much more than the larger one."

The smaller soft penis doesn't become a small hard penis. Usually it will more than double its size when erected. The penis size of most men is slightly more than three and one-half inches in the soft state, and hardens to about six and eight-tenths inches.

While most men more than double their penis size when erected, Masters and Johnson have not found this to be true with men who have a longer than usual soft penis. It will less than double in size, though still tending to be slightly longer than the small soft penis that becomes erect.

"At the moment of truth," Masters and Johnson go on to say, "there just isn't that great differential in size."

This should be turned into a poster and placed on every athletic dressing room and shower door in America.

When all is said and done, your penis is not a penis at all. It's a muscle with the capacity to receive blood that extends it firm and erect. By itself—without your brain of thoughts and feelings—it doesn't have the ability to get hard. When it won't go up, it's not because of a defect or penis inadequacy but due to messages sent to and by your brain. These messages revolve around resentment and lost self esteem.

So it is that masses of young, healthy males in their teens, twenties and thirties, while able to have hard, firm erections when stimulating themselves, are unable to do so when in bed with a woman.

So it is, also, that men in their forties, fifties, sixties or older often say that their sex life is behind them and are convinced that they can no longer, or seldom, have an erection with a woman. They tell themselves that "I've entered life's passage that eliminates erections," when the truth is that forty or more years of resentment has finally diminished their hard penis.

It's crucial, therefore, at all ages, that what you think and feel inside your head doesn't put down the head of your penis. When the ones you love expect you to be right, good and excellent as a condition of love—and you buy into this barter—the resentment you feel about this seeds your rage, rage that eventually blocks your way to getting erections.

Respond to Her, Not Your Penis

Let your thoughts, your self-appraisals and evaluation of her fly out the window. Respond to your erotic, loving feelings for her. Respond to her, the person she is, which includes her physical expressions. Let your feelings take you where they will. Trust them, and in so doing leave your penis out of it. It's then that your penis gets included, fully so. It becomes more than an appendage to be exercised under certain, prescribed, product-centered conditions. You replace performing with making love.

The Big Man Myth

The myth of the big man having a big penis has been dispelled by Masters and Johnson.[109] Truth is, penis length has less of a corresponding relationship to body size than is true of all other body organs. Masters and Johnson found, in their studies, that the man with the longest penis was 5'7", 152 pounds. The shortest penis belonged to a man 5'11", 178 pounds.

Our product-centered world confuses bigness with being the best. Consequently we assume that smaller men suffer more anxiety about themselves. Not necessarily so. The big man whose expectations of himself are based on his size and macho appearance lives in fear of failure. Society handed these expectations to him, and he accepted. "Will I satisfy? Will I measure up? Will I be esteemed and loved when in fact I may not be able to perform the expected products?"

In moments of intimacy with a woman, a time of reckoning must be faced, or so he sees it. The tall, huge man who uses his body to win self esteem invites anxiety about himself and his sexual behavior. His relationships and erections head for a downfall.

IMPACT-CENTERED MEN

The impact-centered man can be identified by a number of unique characteristics. He's like a multi-faceted gem, with some facets flawless, others containing slight fissures, and all sending reflections of his identity in the world without fearfully concealing any of them. When all facets are viewed together, which he is willing to have done, he becomes a total person, capable of loving and being loved for all of who he is. He doesn't guardedly show only the right parts, the good facets, for he has put aside these kinds of evaluations, willing to openly share the full impact of who he is. He's convinced that some of who he is has a more effective impact on himself and other people; other parts don't work as well, but he doesn't feel wrong or bad about this.

The more that he can live in impact-centered ways, the more he can expect to be sexually active throughout his life. Masters and Johnson pointed out that erections continue into the 70's as long as a man believes in himself, in his sexual capability, and has a woman interested in sex.

The Myth of Passages

In exposing ancient myths about sexual behavior, many developmental studies reported in textbooks simply cease to exist. Moreover, "passages" that men and women are expected to pass through become obliterated. A product-centered world, based on controlling your social, personal, sexual and work behavior, insists that you follow passages carefully mapped out for you. These passages need not be followed. Don't let people, books and other prescriptions program you through their passages.

Most passages are culturally defined. They're not biologically determined, not your inevitable destiny. You can choose not to enter passages augered by tradition. New ways of seeing yourself and others can take you out of ruts furrowed by others. Plow your own future.

WOMEN WHO WANT A LARGE PENIS

There's nothing inborn about a woman that would lead her to want an extra large penis. All sorts of experiences can seduce some women, usually when they were young girls, into this wish.

As a growing child, for example, she may have seen her father's penis in either its flaccid or partially hard state, as can occur in routine showering or early morning awakening. Because of this, it being an early experience with her powerful, supportive, loving father, she may have been awed by its size. No matter what its actual dimensions, it may have seemed huge. Thereafter her search for a large penis may continue through life, symbolizing a need for someone with the characteristics — all of them — admired in her father's strength and love.

Moreover, folklore and myths that equate penis size with strength, support and being a man may also influence some women's fantasy wishes. In the newness of her first sexual experience she may recall the penis as huge, regardless of its size. Her search for such a penis — or more accurately, the kind of love feeling associated with the first experience—may continue into future relationships.

Typically, women don't live with a super-huge penis wish, though it does occur. Accepting this wish when it does exist, and understanding that it has ancient origins which have nothing to do with you (and often are unrealistic), may help you accept it in the woman you love. Her huge penis wish is normal.

Loving her in a two-way (yours and hers) impact-centered relationship may enable her to give up fantasies of the super penis. At the same time, in an impact-centered relationship, changing this fantasy is neither necessary nor desirable. If distortions and fantasies of this kind don't fade away, they won't impair your relationship.

THE ADJUSTABLE VAGINA

Whatever the size of a penis, in time the vagina automatically enlarges or reduces its own size to clasp it. For most women, therefore, penis size just doesn't matter, as long as you don't present it as a product to her, but as a part of yourself. Variations in sensation and satisfaction are instigated in her head, not her vagina or clitoris. It's here that pleasure is recorded and experienced.

Meaning of the Relationship: Key to Orgasms

Masters and Johnson made remarkable studies of what a woman experiences during sex by placing a camera inside her vagina. They found, to begin with, that her physical reaction to self-masturbation was stronger than when having sex with her husband. Yet, surprisingly, she said that the orgasm with her husband was significantly better than when she had masturbated. She believed it, and so it was. The relationship with her husband had provided a different MEANING to the orgasm, a level of satisfaction beyond scientific measurement.

You Need Not Put On A Penis Performance

Even the most well-meaning, outstanding scientists who have contributed so much to the advancement of human sexuality, speak of sexual activity as a performance. It's said that one "can or cannot perform." It's like a play in several acts, to learn and recite before an audience. When you experience sex as a performance your penis is given the lead role. In front of an audience it becomes vulnerable to stage-fright. What will my reviews be? Will I star? Get a return engagement? Get top billing? How will the performance be? What will the reviews be? Will I be a hard act to follow? Will I let her down? Will my performance be adequate?

As in so much of what we do our worst critic is ourselves. We've learned well the lessons on how to evaluate oneself. In our humanness, our fragile inconsistencies, unrecognized impulses, perplexing and suddenly unexpected needs, there's plenty of opportunity to label ourselves wrong and bad, if this is the report card system we're going to use. In an impact-centered world there's no room for Academy Awards. As Woody Allen has noted, there isn't THE best. There are segments of each hour or day or life that are effective and may have terrific impact on emotions and thoughts of others. Other parts may work less effectively, not get the job done like we had wanted it, but we're not left with a sense of having lost the Academy Award of self esteem.

DON'T LET THEM DESTROY YOUR SEX LIFE

Your Resentment Can Ruin Your Sex Life

One of every two marriages is in trouble sexually.[110] But sexual troubles start long before marriage takes place. It begins in childhood, even infancy, reaching advanced stages during teenage years. In fact, the most often heard complaint by males at health centers in the nation's universities is sexual impotence.[111] Masses of college age men throughout America are unable to get an erection when needed in bed with a woman.

Filled with unconscious resentment at having to perform — to be "good" — fearful of not measuring up in the eyes of a woman, anxious about doing it right, not wrong, unconscious thoughts cut off the blood supply to their penis. They're left with limp self esteem. They feel put down in the eyes of the woman and themselves.

Masturbation: Their Fears Tried to Cheat You From It

Very early in your life you began to enjoy your body, but were promptly given cues that this was shameful. Their subtle messages said that it wasn't allowed. There was something wrong, not right, about it, and when you stimulated yourself you, your person, also were wrong. Indeed you were bad.

In spite of what your culture taught you, nature usually won out, especially when it came to masturbating, in the case of males. Most males and many females masturbate in direct ways. Some do it subtly, especially females at early ages, and aren't aware of what they are doing. Masturbation is here to stay, and no codes, directives, threats or moralizing of any kind are going to stamp it out.

Masturbation is any sort of stimulation that results in erotic arousal. On the one hand it's a universal experience of intense pleasure and, on the other, a basis of rejection, guilt and loss of self esteem. In infancy males express erotic feelings at many levels, including erections. Some males, in fact, are born with an erection. Young females also find ways of stimulating themselves, such as rubbing their legs together.

Many girls are subtly taught that self-stimulation is wrong, and eventually they give it up. Later, as adults, they cannot recall their earlier masturbation activities.

Girls Who Don't Know They Have a Vagina

In the beginning, very young girls are interested in their vagina.[112] This makes sense. Their vagina is part of them, belongs to them and, like any other part of their body, deserves attention. In the process of becoming acquainted with their vagina, they're stimulated. Pleasure at this upsets adults, however, and efforts are made to distract them. In countless unspoken ways young girls are taught that genital pleasure is wrong, and they're left with a sense of being a bad person. So it is that girls learn to stay away from their vagina, even though it is a part of who they are.

Many begin to deny that it exists at all. Often, not until adolescence do they realize that they have a vagina. It is not uncommon for them to confuse their urethra with their vagina, thinking that it is somehow connected with having babies.

Masturbation Guilt Interferes With Later Sex Relationships

Few behaviors are so widely rejected as genital stimulation. The results are guilt and lost self esteem, with the effects lasting a lifetime. This is starting to change, however. Women's magazines and popular books written in everyday, interesting language are opening doors to their own bodies, with new attitudes about them. Not only are women discovering their clitoris, but are learning about its value, pleasure and usefulness without having to feel wrong about any of it.

Almost as many kinds of masturbation exist as there are women. Some reach orgasms by stimulating their breasts, some by stroking the clitoris, others when rubbing areas of the vagina. In some instances women find less recognized areas, like a spot on their back, which may arouse them and lead to an orgasm. For a few women sexual fantasies are sufficient.

The Center of Your Orgasms

For years controversy focused on which was better, a "vaginal" or "clitoral" orgasm? It became an object of more product-centered sex, another dimension on which to rate women as right or wrong, good or bad, and keep them under control.

Thanks again to Masters and Johnson, we now know that regardless of what stimulation precedes it, there's only one kind of orgasm. It takes place only in the vagina. When an orgasm is brought on by directly stimulating the clitoris, the same sort of reactions happen in the vagina as when an orgasm occurs while a penis is in the vagina. Women no longer need be harnessed by myths which say they are inadequate if their orgasm happens without vaginal stimulation. They are "complete women" whatever the sequence of events leading to their orgasms.

TAKING YOUR ORGASMS OFF THE MARKET

Taking Your Orgasms Out of Boxes

When you have preconceived notions about what kind of product your orgasm—and your partner's—should be, you may be in trouble. Marriage manuals, folklore, myths and party-talk have put orgasms in fancy containers. They're labeled as desirable, multiple, single, faked, wild, mild and on into the night.

Men and women strive for the *best*. They want to *satisfy*. They want it to be *good*. They want it to be *better* than it ever was with anyone else.

"Best," "good," and "better" are cues that a product-centered way of viewing sex, or anything else, is taking place. The want to "be a man." They want to be "a complete woman." They validate themselves as men and women according to how good, better or best their products are purchased in the marketplace of the bedroom.

Throw Away Your Score Card

As long as you think of your ejaculations as signs of "being a man" rather than a male, eventually you'll suffer lowered self-estimations of yourself. As a male — a biologically determined organism — you can expect that at about age 30 you'll no longer ejaculate more than once during sex. This has been described as evidence of "diminishing powers."[113]

This passage is not a biological fact of life. Instead, those men who enter it appear to do so as a result of their experiences, how they see themselves, along with simply following what the culture has prescribed for them.

While more than one ejaculation, or 'coming,' in making love to a woman is by no means necessarily desirable, you need not be limited to a single one for biological reasons after age 30 or even 40. More often the single ejaculation is, in the 30's and 40's, more a matter of self esteem problems, resentment and self-reproach. The fact is that you as a person, a man, beyond being a male, are as potent as ever.

While your biology may change with age, changes in self esteem, attractiveness to women and being loved need not alter at all. Nothing, not even an aging biology, affects sexual behavior as fully as your self esteem. As long as your self-estimation remains high, resentment will not become an interfering agent, and your sexual interest, drive and orgasms will continue.

A Woman's Propensity for Orgasms

While most men have a single orgasm most women are potentially multi-orgasmic. Her several orgasms that follow the first one aren't merely aftershocks. Within minutes she may climax four or five times and experiences each one more satisfying than the first. These many orgasms don't make the score 5 to 1, she wins.

Furthermore, the woman's propensity for several orgasms as a reaction to a single sequence of love making may continue far past age 30, sometimes into her 60's. Many women, living in darkness of undiscovered freedom from right and wrong, do not fully discover their sexuality until their 30's or 40's, and it is then that multiple orgasms are released. Only a product-centered, good-bad focused man will see orgasms as an adequacy contest.

Sexual Potency During Your Second Half Century

What the research seems to be saying, along with clinical evidence, persons who can reasonably well replace a right-wrong, good-bad existence with an impact focus during their 20's, 30's and beyond, can retain maximum vigor throughout their first half century of living, with a fully enjoyable sexual life well into their 70's.

This doesn't ordinarily happen, however, because so few members of society relate to themselves on an impact basis. Their product-centered, right-wrong way of seeing themselves undermines their physiology, particularly the sexual drive, by resentment. By age 30 many of these product-centered victims observe their erections take a downhill turn. Whatever else you thought, your erections aren't in the head of your penis, but in the head above your shoulders. What happens there determines your erections. Like it or not, your brain controls your penis.

However it's easy to blame physical reasons rather than your thoughts for inability to have an erection. For example, at least until recently complaints about not having erections came more from the age group of the 30's and, especially, the 40's and 50's, since they report sometimes drastic losses in frequent or regular erections in sex. Many physicians who, themselves, live a good-bad, product-centered life hear the complaints of their male patients and, as well, notice their own erection losses. It becomes easy to write this change off to aging.

Resentment and Lost Self Esteem, Not Aging, Reduces Erections

Aging itself is not the culprit. It's having aged in a social environment that breeds resentment and destroys self esteem. Anger against those who capriciously regard your self-worth on a right-wrong basis of evaluation, eventually gets turned inward — by your own doing — upon self. Your sexual arousal system and organs become innocent victims of buried rage.

While resentment and self-depreciation are largely responsible for early diminution of sexual activity, another force is at work. We've all heard about built-in obsolescence of the electric light bulb. Well, society also builds in "sexual obsolescence."

Fading male sexual responsiveness at 30, diminishing considerably in the 40's and 50's, are predetermined for many men by cultural expectations. You are taught to expect reduced sexual activity. This makes it simple, not only to follow society's prescription, but to explain your "lost drive." How else can it make sense, since the reason for reduced sexual drive has been carefully repressed in unconscious resentment.

Your Sex Life IS Different Than Animals

Your sexuality, unlike that of animals, is in the wiring of your mind, not in the bulb. The human bulb will last a lifetime. It's connected to the wiring of your higher brain centers — centers that animals don't have.

These centers need only be turned on by your sexual interest and loving responses to another interested human being. No great rush of hormones is necessary. Only the presence of *some* hormones working in a friendly atmosphere, free of resentment and in consortium with self esteem, are all that's required.

Thoughts and Feelings Control Your Chemistry

Men whose sexual activity has lessened are sometimes given hormone treatments. In some cases, sexual interest, arousal and activity pick up. It's not unusual, however, for increased sexual behavior to soon diminish, even though on a continued schedule of treatment with hormones.

It's almost as if in the beginning of treatment added hormones in the body act as a physiological reminder of earlier years when drive was high and uninhibited by resentment.

WHEN HIGH FREQUENCY SEX
IS A SYMPTOM OF IMPOTENCY

Some persons may be impotent even though day after day they have many orgasms. Full personal satisfaction is never really felt, however; there's only fatigue. The need to stop, rest or go to sleep may not be accompanied by a sense of wholeness, satiation or loving completion.

"The neurotic suffers an incapacity for satisfaction," Dr. Fenichel tells us, and becomes "orgastically impotent."[114]

It's an irony, therefore, that some sexually very active men and women who have great numbers of orgasms are sexually inadequate. Sex becomes something outside themselves. Being sexually separated from their own bodies, they're unable to get inner satisfaction. Their high production of orgasms becomes meaningless. Their need for a deep relationship remains unfulfilled, empty. They deny themselves and others the deeper, fuller regions of their person. They "can't get enough." What is missing, however, is not sexual satisfaction, but a deep relationship without good or bad in it, free of self-demeaning attitudes.

PART SIX

YOU ARE NOT HELPLESS

To be something
One must do something.

YOU CAN BEGIN NOW

You may be putting up with your present unrewarding lifestyle because you're convinced that there's nothing you can do about it. Nonsense. You CAN do something. True, you've been harnessed by others, but freedom from their critical attitudes and expectations is possible.

You can put aside your need for praise, trying to be right and getting love as a reward for being a good person. You can begin immediately to behave toward yourself and others in IMPACT centered ways, expressing the you that nobody knows, becoming the person you've always been but have cautiously concealed from yourself.

WHAT RIGHT AND WRONG, GOOD AND BAD REALLY MEAN

Right-wrong, good-bad are moralistic labels invented to control your behavior. When told that something you've thought, felt or done is good, you pleasurably feel like a good person. For the moment you feel safe. People, you've noticed, don't ordinarily harm, shame, or discard individuals who are labeled "good."

At the moment of "feeling good," at some deeper level you are usually apprehensive. Though personally safe for the time, your status could change. Since human beings are imperfect, subject to the whims of chance and their own limitations, what you do in the future may not be labeled right and good.

Also, "right" and "good" behavior judgments vary from person to person. You simply can't please everyone all the time. Your self esteem and belief in yourself as lovable, therefore, are placed in serious jeopardy.

Resentment toward those who parcel out self esteem and love leaves you anxious, even guilty. Unconsciously you turn these feelings into disguised rage toward them, your self and your body. Relationships become impaired, making you vulnerable to illnesses.

In this book you've discovered that people of ancient times, living without the science of understanding human behavior, accidentally stumbled onto the discovery that making people feel "good" or "bad" about themselves was a powerful way of getting them to do things "right." It's easy to see why society continues to be oblivious to destructive effects that "right" and "good" have on people.

Using these labels seems so logical and has become the armament of millions around the world; therefore few question its usefulness. In fact to do otherwise sets one up for severe criticism.

STEPS TO BECOMING IMPACT CENTERED

How do you free yourself of product-centered relationships? How do you become IMPACT centered, no longer putting aside your happiness, refusing to cheat yourself of enduring, deep relationships and a full life-expectancy?

There are no magic formulas, astrological charts, ESP or words whispered by creatures from outer space. However, there are steps, ones that lead you toward self esteem and enduring realistic love relationships that extend emotional well-being and physical health.

STEP 1.

GETTING RID OF THE NEED
FOR YOU AND OTHERS
TO BE "RIGHT"

Whether or not aware of it, you've always fastened some measure of "rightness" to what you've thought, felt and done. "How right was I?" "Was that the right sort of thing to think?" "Are these the right kinds of feelings I'm having?" "Did I have the right intentions?"

Automatically, with the unseen speed of a computer, you have been taught to give each thought, feeling or act an A or A-, or B, or C, or D, or F. Most of your self-report-card grading is done on matters so routine that you hardly notice. Only in larger, more critical matters, perhaps while in front of observers at school or work, are you distinctly aware of self-judgments regarding your adequacy. It always seems necessary to measure up. The need to be right still rules your life, and you resent it. Now, however, you can change this.

Taking 'Right' Out of Your Life

When you decide to become IMPACT centered, you no longer find pleasure in hearing them say:

You've said it *right*.

You've written it *right*.

You've read it *right*.

You've understood it *right*.

You've done it *right*.

You've had the *right* intentions.

You've had the *right* thoughts.

You've had the *right* sort of feelings.

You've cared for your body
in the *right* ways.

Take "right" out of your life. It's a relic of antiquity, dangerous to your happiness and health, and certain to eat away at your love relationships. You don't need it.

IMPACT CENTERED QUESTIONS

Being IMPACT centered you ask yourself any one or more of the following questions:

1. What impact, or effects, did my product — what I did — have on me?

2. What impact did my product have on someone else?

3. What impact did my product have on objects and events in the world?

When you look at the effects your behavior has had on you, without asking, "Was it right?" or "Did I do good?" some remarkably different things happen. To begin with, you no longer need fear that you may not be a "good person." You don't require yourself to be right, since you know that "right" is a fiction that has outlived its usefulness. Consequently, anxiety about being right and good melts away.

Not being anxious you can focus your attention, sustain concentration on whatever it is you're doing, realistically size up any situation confronting you. Unafraid of having to be right, you can behave spontaneously. You are no longer encased in cautious behavior. You have an easy, back and forth flow of thoughts between your unconscious self and your aware self. Rigid walls no longer separate unacceptable thoughts and feelings that you used to believe were "not right" and made you a bad person. Unfearful of what goes on between the inner regions of your brain, you can think, feel and act spontaneously.

You liberate your creative self in this way, live life more fully, and become interesting, even exciting for others to experience.

Furthermore, since it's no longer necessary to be "right" according to someone else's standards, resentment disappears. Divesting yourself of anger and its inevitable long-term consequences turned against those you love and your body, you make life more consistently satisfying. Moreover, you can realistically hope for a deep relationship that will "last forever."

SUBSTITUTE "DID IT WORK?"
FOR "WAS IT RIGHT?"

When you ask, "What impact did my behavior have?" you simply mean "Did it work? Did it get the job done that I intended?"

You may find, upon examination, that what you did got the job done effectively. It — your behavior — accomplished what you set out to do.

For example, predicting it would rain one morning, even though others reminded you that there wasn't a cloud in the sky, you carried your umbrella. Later it did rain. From an impact centered point of view, you hadn't been "right." Instead you had made some judgments — which in this case were your products — that turned out to be accurate. What you predicted, that is what you did, *worked* for you. Furthermore your friends who chided your prediction aren't thought of as 'wrong'; their judgments just didn't work. You remained dry. They got wet.

In not thinking of yourself as "right" you escape from seeing yourself as a good person. You no longer have to live your life trying to be right, freeing yourself to be creative, spontaneous and tap your full wealth of previously untapped personal resources. This frees you of crippling resentment that is an inevitable outcome of having to be the right kind of person like others want. They also win, since your freedom from resentment makes it possible for you to fully identify with humankind in a positive way, enhancing your constructive behavior and eliminating destructive impulses toward others and yourself.

Using another kind of example of impact evaluation, let's suppose that while driving your automobile you exceeded the speed limit and were given a traffic violation ticket. In this case your behavior product — what you did — DIDN'T WORK FOR YOU. You were not bad or wrong. The traffic violation resulted in a financial loss, perhaps lost time in traffic court and other losses.

In realistically appraising the impact of your behavior, how effectively it worked or not, free of moralistic labels that only create anxiety and guilt which promote resentment, you identify with society, work toward its ends. And you, yourself, are facilitated.

In Summary
Examine what you think, feel and do from a point of view that asks:

Did it work for me?

Did it get the job done?

Do I feel comfortable with it?

Do they understand what I wanted them to understand?

Did they respond with behavior that I had hoped for?

Did it make our relationship a more satisfactory, rewarding one?

Did it bring us closer together, develop trust, loyalty, commitment or any other outcome that I aimed toward?

Did it move me a step closer to my goal, whether in understanding mathematics, getting a job, winning a contest, eliciting affection, interest or whatever?

163

The "Did It Work?" Question
Protects Society

When your product, what you do, hurts or damages other people, then the "Did it work?" question must be answered, "No, it DIDN'T work." When society is attacked it strikes back. Therefore products that work against people are ineffective and consequently work against you.

This protects you and members of society. Free of anxiety, guilt and deeply buried resentment that gets expressed in disguised rage, you no longer sabotage society's need to work together in harmonious ways.

You win —

AND SOCIETY WINS!

The outcome, as we have seen in endless statistics describing our destructive society, is quite different. Today, as it has been for several thousand years, humankind controls one another with rights and wrongs, goods and bads, and the results are devastating.

When you refuse to any longer evaluate yourself and others with archaic moralistic labels invented to strike fear into you, you've removed a fiction from your life that makes consistent happiness and general health possible. The world will not, does not fall apart or sink into evil and uncontrollable impulses. On the contrary, this makes possible the kind of world that the inventors of moralistic controls hoped for but have never accomplished. Their purposes have been noble enough; the means of achieving them have simply promoted a chronic epidemic of wasted personal lives, unncessary illnesses and premature death.

STEP 2.

GETTING RID OF SEEING YOURSELF
AND OTHERS
AS BEING 'WRONG' ABOUT ANYTHING

In the same way that no thought, feeling or act is right, it is also true that nothing is "wrong." Wrong is merely a label fastened onto a product after the fact. It's a judgment and nothing more; it has no reality of its own.

Yet teachers, parents and others have discovered the power of labeling a spelling paper, a child's behavior or friend's actions as wrong. "Wrong" has moralistic power that reduces self esteem and diminishes your feeling of being lovable. Over the centuries, in subtle, imperceptible ways "wrong" came to mean "bad."

Sometimes you are a "little wrong," other times "very much wrong." Depending on what kind of product is being judged, as well as the times and person doing the evaluating, you may feel "kinda bad" or "very bad," according to the degree you've been labled wrong. Mostly, however, you feel only a little bad, since much of what you do is of small dimensions. These "little bads" are felt though, generally just below the surface of awareness, and they add up. Over the years, the constant bombardment of wrongs and bads begin to carve a negative picture of yourself, denying self esteem that's required for healthy living.

Taking "Wrong" Out
of Your Life

When you become impact centered you will no longer need to say:

Your answer is *wrong*.

I have the *wrong* idea.

It's *wrong* to do that.

I turned in the *wrong* direction.

It's *wrong* to feel that way.

You put the toy together *wrong*.

You spelled it *wrong*.

Your math problem is *wrong*.

You came the *wrong* time.

Take wrong out of your life. Become aware that no matter how innocent this word seems to be, it disguises a sense of being "bad" associated with it. Know that "wrong" that's used in any way carries "badness" with it.

SUBSTITUTE "IT DIDN'T WORK" FOR "IT WAS WRONG"

If you no longer label behavior as wrong, what do you call it? What do you say?

Look at it, what you do, as ineffective, not wrong. It simply DIDN'T WORK. It was inaccurate, didn't communicate, didn't get done what you intended. Whatever labels you use, if they're moralistic, know that they don't work. Worse, in the long run they turn out to be destructive.

When anything you do isn't wrong it becomes impossible to be a bad person. Without the threat of being called wrong or bad, it's easier to maintain a constant level of self esteem. There's no need, consequently, to strike back at people who lower self-estimation. Your life becomes less anxiety and guilt ridden. You can get about the business of contented, happy, fully actualized living.

Other Benefits
of Impact Evaluation

When you replace "I was wrong" with "It didn't work," not only can you better maintain self esteem but opportunities open up to grow from the experience. This can happen as a result of other impact questions that you can ask:

To what extent didn't it work?

At what point did it stop working?

In what ways didn't it work?

What were the effects on others? on myself?

These kinds of questions get you to openly explore your behavior, searching for ways to make your products work effectively for you.

Substituting impact evaluations of this kind in schools, getting rid of right-wrong, "A" to "F" labels could increase learning to phenomenal levels. The same can happen to you, of course, in all your relationships with life. You can evaluate on much broader, deeper dimensions than traditional evaluations provide.

STEP 3.

GETTING RID OF THE NEED

FOR YOU AND OTHERS

TO BE "GOOD"

Living in impact centered ways it no longer feels pleasurable when they say to you that:

You are a *good* person.

You've done a *good* job.

That's a *good* way of doing it.

It's *good* that you feel that way.

It's a *good* time to do it.

What you say is *good*.

That's a *good* idea.

I have such *good* feelings about you.

You take *good* care of your body.

Have a *good* day.

To even suggest that labeling people "good" or "right" may be deleterious to their health or happiness can be expected to receive derision or, at best, incredulous smiles.

WORDS DO MATTER

You may be saying, "But it's only a matter of semantics. You're simply using other words for good and bad, right and wrong."

Indeed, it IS a matter of semantics. Words DO count. Words are powerful. They move people and nations. Certain words can be spoken and your mouth will water. Other words can make you hungry, stimulate or moisten your genitals, change your respiration, heartbeat, the amount of sugar secreted by your pancreas.

Yes, words — the ones you use — are important! Powerful meanings, influencing how you feel about yourself and how your body functions, whether it stays well or gets sick, become attached to words. In our society, as for centuries in most countries around the world, right and wrong, good and bad have come to have powerful controlling effects on how people feel and think about themselves. Somehow, the behavioral scientists have missed the tremendous importance of these four words and their derivations. Institutionalization of these words covers over their moralistic meaning even when used as ways of conveying accuracy or correctness.

SUBSTITUTE "DID IT WORK?"
FOR "WAS IT GOOD?"

Being impact centered, you explore the effects your behavior has on others and the world of objects (or things) and events. No longer do you ask yourself, "Did I do a good job?" Instead you pose impact questions:

How did it work?

To what extent did it work?

In what ways was it effective?

How could it have been more effective?

What was there about it that made it work?

STEP 4.

GETTING RID OF SEEING YOURSELF

AND OTHERS

AS BEING "BAD"

Just as nothing is in itself wrong, it is also true that no thought, feeling or act is bad. "Bad" is an abstraction; it has no real, concrete existence. It's a label fastened onto behavior, invented to control you with fear about your worth.

What is called bad depends upon the times in which one lives, as well as culture, religious beliefs, and social standards. As we've already seen in this book, wearing a bathing suit that exposed skin above the knee was at one time, not too long ago, considered wrong and could get you arrested.

As in the case of "wrong," "bad" is a fiction, a device intended to control you through guilt and fear of losing self esteem and love.

Whatever immediate, positive results, the long-term impact is a disaster. It breaks down relationships, destroys intimacy and sexual response. You're left vulnerable to disease and death long before your cells, tissues and organs would otherwise wear out.

Removing "Bad" From Your Life

When you elect to live with yourself and others in impact centered ways,

you will no longer say:

What you've done is *bad.*

That's a *bad* way of thinking about it.

Those are *bad* thoughts.

It's a *bad* time to raise that issue.

It's a *bad* way of looking at it.

You behaved *badly.*

Those are *bad* feelings.

You've treated your body *badly.*

STEP 5.

LOOKING AT THE IMPACT
YOUR PRODUCTS HAVE HAD
ON
THOUGHTS, FEELINGS, ACTS
AND THE WORLD

After you're used to asking the "Did it work?" question, you can begin to apply it to your thoughts, feelings and the things you do. You can also apply it to the world of objects and events.

Impact of Your Products on Thoughts

Not only do you ask, "Did it work?" but also "What effects did my products have on my thoughts?" In other words, whether it was a a picture you painted, a dinner prepared, game played or any other performance, you would ask yourself:

> How is my THINKING influenced or changed as a result of what I did? Do I now have new IDEAS? Have my THOUGHTS changed as a result of the product I produced?

In replacing, "Was it right? Was it wrong? Was it good? Was it bad?" with searching for the IMPACT of your behavior on your thoughts, you don't end with a "yes" or "no" to moralistic questions.

You invite yourself, instead, to thoughtfully learn from your own product, expanding not only what you accomplished but your future behavior. Moralisms are replaced by analyzing, synthesizing and searching for new answers. You become your own teacher, finding your own solutions to life.

Moreover, you search for feedback on how 'what you did' affected the thoughts of other people:

> When I produced my product, how did I affect your thinking? What ideas came into your mind? Did you have any new thoughts — ideas you've never had before? Did my product send your thinking into an area unrelated to my product?

Feedback of this kind can provide you with far more growth than simply labeling what you did as right or wrong, good or bad. Not only do you learn more, embellishing yourself, but you aren't left feeling resentful for having been under the control of someone promising to praise you.

Impact of Your Product On Your Feelings and Those of Others

After producing a product, not only do you evaluate its impact on thoughts but also on FEELINGS:

> What feelings did I have as I was producing the product? How did these feelings affect what I was doing? What new or strange feelings did I experience? Now that I look back on the experience and my product, what feelings do I have now? What do these feelings tell me? What can I learn from

them? How can I be even more effective in my products, using what I know now about my feelings?

Furthermore, whenever possible or if it seems useful, you get feedback about feelings your product generated in other people:

What feelings did you find yourself having as I was producing my product? What feelings do you have now? Were your feelings intense, unusual, surprising, frightening? Did they motivate you in any way? Inspire you? Turn you off?

Again it becomes obvious that with this kind of feedback you begin to get a broader, deeper picture of how effectively or not your product has communicated, than is true when using a simplistic label of right or wrong. You discover what works, when, where, why and how it works or not. You enlarge your understanding and better prepare yourself for future behavior.

STEP 6.

BECOMING IMPACT CENTERED
BY DOING WHAT YOU ALREADY KNOW
HOW TO DO

You and the Beanstalk

Like people, beans have a rhythm of sleeping and "being awake."

That is, there's a systematic, rhythmic sequence of growing and not growing that beans follow. However, if beans are kept perpetually in the dark, they don't develop this rhythm. Curiously, though, if exposed to light for only one very brief period, they'll begin a twenty-four-hour rhythm of sleeping and not sleeping, even when returned to darkness. This liberated propensity for movement remains with them throughout their lifetime.[115]

You as well have all the propensities necessary for growth and new behavior, ways of living your life like you want to but always thought you couldn't. If for even a brief period of time you expose the potential you've cautiously held back, you can change your life around.

Releasing your spontaneous, creative, even charismatic self, you no longer need to live in dark shadows cast by others that curtail your potential.

YOU ARE WHAT YOU DO

All that you are doesn't exist until you act on it. You are what you do. Were you to think nothing, feel nothing, do nothing, you would be little more than a vegetable. It's in the DOING that makes you who you are. You become someone by doing something. The kind of someone you are depends on what you do.

This isn't a common point of view. Most people mistakenly think that first your personality must change and then your new behavior follows. For example most would think, "He's an outgoing person. That's why he behaves in extrovertive ways." This simply isn't true. The friendly, open person behaves often enough in ways that are identified as outgoing, so that eventually this individual is thought of by others as a sociable person. Often repeating friendly behavior, the individual does, in fact, become outgoing.

Getting rid of right and wrong, good and bad from your life seems like a simple undertaking. It is. It's simple but not easy. In time, however, struggling to undo the past, rearranging how people have taught you to evaluate yourself, you will find that you CAN become someone who:

> Sees yourself in IMPACT centered ways, free of evaluating what you think, feel and do as right or wrong, good or bad and thereby let your spontaneous, creative, charismatic self emerge in your social, personal and intimate relationships.

THAT'S IT

Yes, that's IT! It's that simple—and that difficult! Simple because you ALREADY know how to do what needs to be done; difficult because you aren't used to behaving in ways other than those that fit a measuring scale of right to wrong, good to bad.

Erasing Your Long History of Right and Wrong

Your entire life and the lives of everyone you know have been spent thinking, feeling and doing the sort of things that win recognition for you, enhance your self esteem and make it possible to be attractive and loved. This behavior is reasonable, because it's all you've known. It's also about the only way that anyone relates to you. It all has become a part of you, ingrained from almost your first year or two. Years of trying to behave in the right ways in order to be loved have turned you into a product-centered person, unconsciously preoccupied with trying to produce product behavior that's right and good, not wrong and bad.

You'll find that to change this will feel as if you're giving up something precious, indeed replacing the very core of who you are. You'll notice yourself tenaciously clinging to the old ways of seeing yourself —as right or wrong, arguing for the sensibleness of good and bad as a way of seeing yourself and others. You'll experience an urge to defend using right and wrong, even though this book points out the endless misery and destruction wrought by this method to control each other and teach our young.

It's important to become aware of your resistance, for this awareness can help you see your enemy and turn in new directions. Simple as impact living is, it's the familiarity of the old, traditional methods of evaluating yourself that gets in the way. We do not easily give up what we are used to, even when it works against our personal happiness and health.

You're also convinced that you cannot be spontaneous. Under-evaluating yourself seems so much a part of you that to be other than reserved, cautious and unsure seems to be a hopeless task. It's not. You CAN free the old, guarded uninteresting you.

JUST BELOW YOUR SURFACE SELF
IS YOUR CHARISMATIC YOU

Your task isn't to learn how to be creative, spontaneous and charismatic. You already know how to be the kind of person you want to be. When you relinquish present ways of trying to win self esteem, making right and wrong obsolete, you'll no longer hold back the healthier, spontaneous you. Your human rights to living all of you will be met.

YOU CAN CHOOSE NOT TO SUFFER

Psychologist and best-selling author, Dr. Harold Greenwald, reminds us that:

> If you are convinced that you are a sufferer you can either choose to continue suffering because of the many payoffs it brings you, or you can choose to *act* cheerful and soon you will probably find you *are* cheerful.[116]

Dr. Greenwald extends this thought to all facets of your life. By DOING what you would like TO BE, making a "direct decision," as he would say, to act the kind of person you want to live, you become that person!

The key decision to being impact centered is to recognize right and wrong, good and bad as outworn, obsolete methods of controlling yourself and others. You already know how to unshackle yourself from these fearsome controls and, in their place, substitute methods that tell you about your impact on the world. All that's left for you to do is KNOW this and begin to ACT on it.

When What's Simple Becomes Profound

Simplistic, you say. While we tend to distrust what is simple, especially if it solves large problems, history has demonstrated time and again that more often than not solutions to vexing problems prove to be simple—when they're finally uncovered.

For example, after many would-be inventors tried to get a heavier than air vehicle to fly, with countless efforts to emulate birds ending in failure, the Wright brothers combined some simple observations and got the job done. An uncomplicated wing design for lift and a propeller for pull got their ambitions off the ground.

One of the simplest machines we have today — used perhaps more than any other — is the paperclip. Each day, in every town, it works for us, holding our papers together. Although of simple design it took centuries to be conceived.

Still another illustration. The idea or "theory" of germs is also simple, especially now that we recognize the role these tiny organisms have in disease. It wasn't always this way. When first proposed that these creatures, too small to be seen with the naked eye, existed, the whole notion was stamped preposterous. . The idea of controlling illnesses, epidemics and death by keeping germs from spreading among people was scoffed at when first introduced.

When tried, however, the "germ theory" did indeed work. Removing the common drinking cup from the town pump, using drinking fountains without placing your mouth on them, and resorting to throw-away paper cups, all made remarkable progress toward reducing disease. Ridding ourselves of moralistic labels of control can have equally profound effects, with a whole new personal happiness and life-span made possible.

RECOGNIZING THAT FREEDOM IS YOUR DECISION

A group of scientists strapped dogs into a harness and gave them shocks which, though not severe, were painfully disturbing, enough so to make them want to escape.[117] Their harness prevented this, of course, and they howled in discomfort.

Later, after many such shocks, the dogs were placed unharnessed into the same box. Again they were shocked. Free of their constricting harness they could now jump over a simple barrier into freedom from pain. But they did nothing. Instead, they howled, urinated, emptied their bowels, and wildly jumped about.

In other words these animals didn't choose to act differently. They did nothing about their problems. Free to change, act in new ways, eliminating pain, they preferred what was familiar. Eventually they stopped howling and running about, settled down and absorbed the pain. They whined quietly.

They didn't require therapy. There was no need for a magical cure, a mysterious force or loving parent to save them. They could have done it themselves. They already had the capacity to run, jump, explore, try out, search and seek. All that was needed — it was this simple!—was to act in different ways, ways they already knew about.

Mental Blinders Narrow Vision

The dogs had lived too long in a harness and now, when they could have done something about the pain in their lives, they were convinced that nothing could be done. They needlessly accepted what they believed to be their fate. So it is among humankind. Harnessed by people's expectations of right and good, they settle into routines of unfulfilled love and lost self esteem. Many find life miserable. A few other poor souls fare slightly better, living their lives in mediocre, uninteresting predictable dullness. Only a handful enjoy their own spontaneity, free of right and wrong, and richly experience the impact they have on the world.

Those Who Have Never Been Harnessed

The same scientists who had shocked dogs in harnesses also studied dogs that had never been harnessed. These animals, having never been forced to endure being strapped-in and pained, thought of the world as a place of choices, and they behaved differently when shocked. When electricity was turned on they jumped about, changed positions and *walked across a barrier to a more satisfying, pleasurable place in life.*

They escaped their pain — as you can — by ACTING, by DOING SOMETHING about it. They did what the other, previously harnessed dogs could have done but chose not to.

Notice that they *didn't have to change themselves.* They stayed the same. They merely began to use what they already knew how to do. The animals already knew how to walk, were acquainted with changing their position, and so didn't require being taught anything new. It was all in the DOING. To change, to become free of your cautious, repressed, low self-estimation self, you need but behave in freeing ways. Behave like the person you want to be, like the person already there, just beneath your surface self.

The earlier dogs, ones who had been harnessed, elected not to get out of their predicament and enjoy life. They chose this *even though finally unharnessed and free to walk over a slight barrier into another part of the box that was free of electricity.* They continued their unnecessary suffering of pain.

No Need to Change, Simply Act In New Ways

So it is that you, as well, needn't learn anything you don't already know. By choosing to do so you can free the spontaneous you that has quietly lived for years with hidden resentment.

It's your choice. You can begin to evaluate yourself — your feelings, thoughts and actions, and those of others — in new ways. By doing so you will reduce guilt, anxiety and fear that has such a significant role in eroding personal relationships and health. By choosing to do so you can free the spontaneous you that has quietly lived for years with hidden resentment and rage.

You DO have choices you can make and act on but have never elected to do so. It's in these choices, which rid you of seeing yourself and others as having to be right and good in order to be loved, that will — simple as it may seem! — turn your life around.

GETTING YOUR GOAT

Dr. Liddle and his associates at Cornell University harnessed a goat on a grid, or wire fence-like floor. When they turned on the electricity the goat felt a mild shock of pain. The experimenters taught him that when he lifted one leg they would turn off the electricity.

Later, free to roam around in the outside world of the barnyard, the goat eventually, by chance, got near a wire fence. It immediately stopped, lifted one leg and froze in that position. He did this every time even though having never been shocked in the barnyard. In fact the barnyard fence hadn't been rigged to carry electricity.

To the surprise of experimenters, the goat had learned to react to ANY wire-like fencing material in the same rigid way as it had in the experimental laboratory. They soon found that other goats who had been shocked on electric wire grids also acted in the same way when in the barnyard.

The goats had learned to act toward life in rigid, tightly closed ways. All wire-like material became a sign of danger. Free to be spontaneous in the barnyard world, to walk, run about and behave in free-ing ways, they surrendered themselves to a paralyzed, unrewarding barnyard life. We call this "neurotic" behavior, because it was un-realistic to behave toward the barnyard fence as if it were an electric-ally charged wire grid.

FENCED-IN RELATIONSHIPS

So it is with people. They experience the shock of good and bad during their early years, suffering lost self esteem. This begins with parents and extends into the future with other authority figures, such as teachers, professors, and bosses at work. Many times a husband or wife is reacted to as an authority figure of this type, always having the potential threat of administering painful "rights," "wrongs," "goods" and "bads." It is often expected that these persons will behave like Later Mother.

You ARE Different Than Animals

Helpful as animal research is, there comes a point where we cannot compare the social-psychological behavior of animals with human be-ings.[118,119] One important difference, indeed monumental, is in the un-conscious reservoir of behavior that characterizes human beings, along with a strict conscience.

Unlike animals, much of your life is directed for you by your un-conscious self. For example, when told that you've been wrong or bad, unlike animals you feel demeaned, unvalued and guilty. This may be so painful that you bury your guilt, repressing it outside of awareness. Subtle or deep depression is the result, weighing heavily on you. It colors your disposition, infringes on relationships and gets in the way of intimacy and sexual satisfaction.

When animals are censored or reprimanded it's soon over and done with. They don't actively reflect on what they've thought or said or done, nor are they introspective. To relieve a sense of guilt they don't resort to defense mechanisms and act out their feelings in disguised ways. People suffer infinitely more from right-wrong, good-bad methods of controlling them. They live their lives with more cortex, higher brain cells, and this humanizes them.

Take the Baton From Their Hands

In the long run, lifting your feet in cadence with tunes played by others as a way of getting self esteem will delay your journey into loving relationships. If you join them in their march, and this can be exhilarating and promote your welfare, simply remove the rights and wrongs of this behavior. Do it because of the impact it has on you and them, impact that isn't evaluated as good or bad.

Marching to the beat of the drummer whose cadence is right-wrong, right-wrong, right-wrong, will evoke resentment in you. You surrender your uniqueness in this kind of cadence, with your spontaneity tightly constricted and hidden in long, even rows that make you only a part of their parade. Synchronized in lock-step fashion, trying to take the "right" steps toward self esteem, you lose your identity.

When you narrow yourself to their moralistic guidelines, the world says that you're "adjusted." You fit. You're a good person. These periodic bits of praise, occasional expressions of affection and scanty scraps of love are temporary solutions to what becomes an insatiable hunger to be loved for the total impact of who you are. Nothing else is available, you think, and however miserable you feel about living this way you settle for it.

Yet nothing could be further from the truth. In finding your way to freedom you no longer need step in tracks left by earlier travelers. You have your own to make, with a stride and imprint that are distinctly your own.

EPILOGUE

A long time ago I discovered that books are not really books at all. They're vehicles for sharing. A person sits somewhere, usually alone at a desk, and shares thoughts, feelings, hopes and dreams. The sharing is mostly with people who can't be reached in any other way.

So it is that, for many years, I've not read a book. Instead, I open up pages and am introduced to a person sharing with me from some distant place. I know the self-discipline required of that person, the hours and sheer effort, energy, anxiety, sometimes drudgery and other times excitement, endured by the writer. Since then I've viewed books differently, approaching them more as persons than inert ink on paper.

This is the way I view the pages here. I call it a book, but only because book is an easy, familiar term. I'm really sharing with you, talking to you about some thoughts I have about you and me.

I particularly appreciate friends who encouraged me to write openly without carefully scrubbing each word, every preposition, with academic soap.

A long time ago, I wrote a newspaper column, "Your Child", for the *Arizona Republic* in Phoenix. The intention was to get outside of academia and communicate with people generally. In it I used incomplete sentences, everyday examples, anything that would communicate. Society editor Maggie Savoy, late of the *Los Angeles Times,* told me that the column turned out to have the most reader interest in its news section. Likewise, I've aimed this book at a wide audience.

In the present volume, the vastly complicated and infinite number of variables that explain human behavior are recognized. Yet the focus is on only a few of these and emphasizes one: the need to be esteemed, valued, obtain touch, affection and love in impact-centered ways, free of right and wrong, good and bad.

In discussing this critical dimension of human functioning, a variety of behaviors are examined. One among these has to do with human intimacy and sexual relationships. Again, some of the classics are referred to here, extending back beyond Havelock Ellis and forward to Kinsey, Pomeroy and Martin, as well as Masters and Johnson, and others.

Today we live on theoretical constructs that are updated versions of theories born in the past. While the original theory may be outdated, at least a few segments of the theory often hold up and are as workable today as yesterday. When not workable, then certainly usable for drawing updated inferences. So it has been that I've borrowed, for example, from Havelock Ellis, Dunbar and others on whose work so many others have built.

It was G. B. Shaw, as I recall, who introduced me to Havelock Ellis' work. At the time, I was at the Phoenix Public Library, then located on Washington Street, to read Ellis. I found him locked in a cabinet. The librarian, with considerable enthusiasm, led me with key in hand to the cabinet, providing me with this "classified" material.

It's of worth to note the distance society has traveled since that time. Ellis, one of the earliest scientists who examined the nature of sexuality in a systematic way, dismissing hearsay about sex, its old wives' tales, taboos and superstitions, had set enlightened forces in motion. Owners of bookstores who sold his books when they first appeared were jailed. During my own teens and twenties, his work was admissible but only under locked-up conditions. Now the locks are gone. The only remaining significant locks today are in one's own mind.

This volume is one of three current books meant to open the way for *Breakthru School*. Along with *Self Esteem In the Classroom* and *Five Ways of Parenting: One That Works!*, it's meant to be an introduction for a breakthrough in education. Breakthru School is not intended as another innovation, nor still another new kind of school, but one meant to make a significant change in the young and tomorrow's society.

Today's society was yesterday's childhood; tomorrow's society is today's childhood. In growing up free of right and wrong, good and bad, esteemed in impact-centered ways, a new world is possible.

BIBLIOGRAPHY

1. Lemmon, Jack. Interview on "Good Morning, America." New York: American Broadcasting Company. Television. April 7, 1978.

2. Rochlin, Gregory. Griefs and Discontents: The Forces of Change. Boston: Little, Brown and Company, 1965. p. 12

3. Kessler, Sheila. Beyond divorce I: divorce counseling technique for professions. In: Courses for People Who Work with People, Spring, 1978: San Diego: University Extension, University of California at San Diego. (Brochure.)

4. Rochlin, Gregory. Griefs and Discontents: The Forces of Change. Boston: Little, Brown and Company, 1965. p. 1

5. Bielski, Robert, and Friedel, Robert. In: The California Medical Association's Western Journal of Medicine, and reported in Parade's Special, by Lloyd Shearer. Parade, July 17, 1977.

6. Zell, John. An invited address to University of Miami-United States Office of Education "TTT" Conference, Coral Gables: University of Miami, 1971.

7. Gorney, Roderic. Conversation with Verne Faust by Roderic Gorney, Psychiatrist-Psychoanalyst, Department of Psychiatry, School of Medicine, University of California at Los Angeles, 1977. (Unpublished.)

8. Dunbar, Flanders. Mind and Body: Psychosomatic Medicine. New York: Random House, 1955. Ninth Printing, 1972.

9. Greer, Stephen. Reported in: "Cancer link to emotions said possible." San Diego: The Evening Tribune, June 7, 1976.

10. James, T.F. "Cancer and your emotions." Cosmopolitan, April, 1960.

11. Friday, Nancy, My Mother/Myself. New York: Dell Publishing Company, 1977. p. 462

12. James, T.F. "Cancer and your emotions." Cosmopolitan, April, 1960.

13. West, Philip. In: "Cancer and your emotions," Cosmopolitan, by T.F. James, April, 1960. p. 41

14. Klopfer, Bruno. "Psychological variables in human cancer." Journal of Projective Techniques, 21, 4, 1957.

15. Rassidakis, N.C. "Schizophrenia and cancer — mutually exclusive?" Psychology Today. November, 1972.

16. Associated Press, San Diego Union. "U.S. crime jumps by 10%." San Diego: The San Diego Union, 1976, p. 1

17. Treffert, Darold. "Fear of Failure Stressed; 'American Fairy Tale' Is Blamed for Suicides Among Youngsters." News release by Assosiated Press writer, 1976.

18. Stolley, Richard. "A crisis worse than anyone could imagine." New York: Life, February 24, 1967.

19. KFI Radio Reporter. News report. Los Angeles: KFI Radio. Unpublished. October 28, 1977.

20. Time Editors. "The law." New York: Time, September, 1976.

21. Starnes, Richard. "Violent crime continues sweep across America." North American Newspaper Alliance. San Diego: San Diego Union, August 8, 1974.

22. Associated Press Reporter. News release. San Diego Union, 1976.

23. Hess, W.R. Diencephalon, Autonomic and Extrapyramidal Functions. New York: Grune and Stratton, 1954.

24. Masserman, Jules. Behavior and Neurosis. Chicago: University of Chicago Press, 1943.

25. Moyer, K.E. "Internal impulses toward aggression." Transactions of the New York Academy of Sciences, 31, 1969.

26. Masserman, J. The Biodynamic Roots of Human Behavior. Springfield, Illinois: Charles C Thomas, 1968.

27. Kavanau, J. "Confinement, adaptation, and compulsory regimes in laboratory studies." Science, 143, 1963.

28. Faust, Verne. The Counselor-Consultant in the Elementary School. Boston: Houghton-Mifflin, 1968.

29. Brunner, Jerome. On Knowing. Cambridge: The Belknap Press of Harvard University, 1962.

30. Arieti, Silvano. The Will to be Human. New York: Quadrangle Books, Inc., 1972.

31. Faust, Verne. Faust Word Association Test (FWAT). San Diego: Thomas Paine Press, 1978.

32. MacLean, Catherine Anne. Repressed Responses to Hate and Sex by Teachers on a Word Association Test. San Diego: United States International University, 1978. Ph.D. dissertation.

33. Azrin, N. "Pain and aggression." In: Readings in Psychology Today. Del Mar, California: CRM Books, 1969.

34. Azrin, N. "Pain and aggression." In: Readings in Psychology Today. Del Mar, California: CRM Books, 1969.

35. Dunlop, E., and Waltmann, R. "The emotional temperature." Psychosomatic Medicine, Proceedings of the First International Congress of the Academy of Psychosomatic Medicine. E. Dunlop, Ed. New York: International Congress Series No. 13; Excepta Medica Foundation, 1967.

36. Levy, S. "Depressive reaction: its diagnosis and treatment with special reference to the 'somatic mask' and the newer psychopharmacologic agents." Psychosomatic Medicine, E. Dunlop, Ed., 1967.

37. NBC News Reporter. National Broadcasting Company news report of Mental Health Commission, April 24, 1972. Unpublished.

38. Masserman, Jules. The Practice of Dynamic Psychiatry. Philadelphia: W.B. Saunders Company, 1955.

39. Nevison, Myrne. "There's another kind of inflation — and the costs are high." Canadian Counselor, 3, 4, October, 1969.

40. Tuohy, William. "World Health Agency zeroes in on suicide." Los Angeles Times, October 25, 1974, Part VI.

41. Rochlin, Gregory. Man's Aggression; the Defense of Self. Boston: Gambit, 1973. pp. 23-51

42. Handen, Herbert. News report. Phoenix, Arizona: Phoenix Gazette. Summer, 1964.

43. United Press International. News Report. Los Angeles Times. Part IV, March 31, 1979. p. 9

44. Gorney, Rod. The Human Agenda. Los Angeles: The Guild Tutors Press. Second Printing, 1979.

45. Sanger, Maury D. The Psyche and Dermatitis. Summit, New Jersey: CIBA Pharmaceutical Products, 1959. Reprint.

46. Tenney, Vivian A. "A clinical study of the psychosomatic aspects of cancer." In: Psychosomatic Medicine; Proceedings of the First International Congress of the Academy of Psychosomatic Medicine, E. Dunlop, Ed. New York, 1967.

47. Shearer, Lloyd. "This machine can save your life." San Diego: Parade, in San Diego Union, September 29, 1974.

48. Lynch, James. The Broken Heart; the Medical Consequences of Lonliness. New York: Basic Books, Inc., 1977. p. 80

49. Zell, John. Phoenix, Arizona: Unpublished conversation, 1977.

50. Glass, Davis C. "Stress, competition and heart attacks." Psychology Today. December, 1976.

51. Greene, William. Reported in: "Heart attack: behavioral disharmony and sudden death." Psychology Today, 1972.

52. Engel, George. Reported in: "Heart attack: behavioral disharmony and sudden death." Psychology Today, 1972.

53. Rochlin, Gregory. Man's Aggression; the Defense of Self. Boston: Gambit, 1973.

54. Parkes, C.M. "The psychosomatic effects of bereavement." In: Modern Trends in Psychosomatic Medicine, O.W. Hill, Ed. New York: Appleton-Century-Crofts, 1970.

55. Lembke, Daryl. "Valium: all is not quiet as use grows." Los Angeles Times. February 11, 1975, Part I.

56. Slovenko, Ralph. Psychiatry and Law. Boston: Little, Brown and Company, 1973.

57. Nevison, Myrne. "Can counseling prevent health costs?" Faculty of Education, University of Ottawa, Canada: Bulletin of the Canadian Guidance and Counseling Association; VIII, 4, January, 1977.

58. Miami Herald. "Killer-drunks can relax — again." The Miami Herald, February 6, 1972.

59. Long, Gaylord. A radio report. California: KSPF-FM Radio. April 2, 1977.

60. Delury, George (Ed.) The World Alamanac and Book of Facts. New York: Newspaper Enterprise Association, 1974.

61. Rader, William. Interview on Merv Griffin Program. Columbia Broadcasting System. August 28, 1974.

62. Smith, Sydney. Report made at Arizona State University, 1945. (Unpublished.)

63. Bartlett, Kay. "Nun found most of her faith in a bottle." Los Angeles Times, December 10, 1078, Part IV. p. 5

64. Snider, Arthur. "The search for sexual fantasy." The Los Angeles Times, December 6, 1978.

65. Slovenko, Ralph. Psychiatry and Law. Boston: Little, Brown and Company, 1973.

66. Galton, Lawrence. "Special treatment for obese children." Parade, February, 1978. (UPI, 1977, A-4)

67. Bruch, Hilda. "Disturbed communication in eating disorders." American Journal of Orthopsychiatry, 33, 1, January 1963.

68. Nelson, Harry, "Pilot studies show promise: wiring jaws shut may be obesity cure of future." Los Angeles Times. October 22, 1977, Part I.

69. Alexander, Franz; French, Thomas, and Pollock, George (Eds.). Psychosomatic Specificity, Volume I, Experimental Study and Results. Chicago: The University of Chicago Press, 1968.

70. Delury, George (Ed.) The World Alamanac and Book of Facts. New York: Newspaper Enterprise Association, 1974.

71. Corbett, Bob. "Diabetes gain made at Scripps." San Diego: The Evening Tribune, November 2, 1977.

72. Dunbar, Flanders. Mind and Body: Psychosomatic Medicine. New York: Random House, 1955. Ninth Printing, 1972.

73. Latham, Aaron. "Hemingway: behind the macho mask, a softer side." Los Angeles Times. October 16, 1977, Part IV, p. 1

74. Dunbar, Flanders. Mind and Body: Psychosomatic Medicine. New York: Random House, 1955. p. 144

75. Englebardt, S.L. "Can accidents be prevented?" Readers Digest, September 1969.

76. Grinker, Roy, and Robbins, Fred. Psychosomatic Casebook. New York: The Blakiston Company, Inc., 1954.

77. Alexander, Franz; French, Thomas; and Pollock, George (Eds.). Psychosomatic Specificity, Volume I, Experimental Study and Results. Chicago: The University of Chicago Press, 1968. p. 12

78. Dunbar, Flanders. Mind and Body: Psychosomatic Medicine. New York: Random House, 1955. pp. 249-53

79. McGrath, William. "Tenesmus of Unwilling Sacrifice." Presentation to the International Academy of Proctology, Fifteenth Annual Teaching Seminar, March 18, 1959.

BIBLIOGRAPHY

80. Alexander, Franz; French, Thomas; and Pollock, George (Eds.). Psychosomatic Specificity, Volume I, Experimental Study and Results. Chicago: The University of Chicago Press, 1968.

81. Greenberg, Samuel. "Neurosis is a painful style of living." Reported in: The VIP Line, The Miami Herald, March 27, 1972.

82. Slovenko, Ralph. Psychiatry and Law. Boston: Little, Brown and Company, 1973.

83. Gorney, Roderic. The Human Agenda. Los Angeles: The Guild Tutors Press. Second Printing, 1979.

84. Gorman, Mike. Every Other Bed. New York: The World Publishing Company, 1956.

85. Nevison, Myrne. "There's another kind of inflation — and the costs are high." Canadian Counselor, 3, 4, October, 1969. p. 55

86. Dunlop, E., and Waltmann, R. "The emotional temperature." Psychosomatic Medicine, Proceedings of the First International Congress of the Academy of Psychosomatic Medicine. E. Dunlop, Ed. New York: International Congress Series No. 13; Excepta Medica Foundation, 1967. p. 195

87. Joint Commission on Mental Illness and Health. Action for Mental Health: Final Report of the Joint Commission on Mental Illness and Health. New York: Basic Books, 1961.

88. Rogow, Arnold. "Some psychiatric aspects of political science and political life." Social Psychology and Political Behavior: Problems and Prospects. Gilbert Abcarian and John Soule, Eds. Columbus Ohio: Charles E. Merrill, 1971.

89. Mills, Enid. Living with Mental Illness. London: Routledge and Kegan Paul, 1962.

90. Gorman, Mike. Every Other Bed. New York: The World Publishing Company, 1956.

91. Miller, A., and Wexler, P. "Utilization of Manpower in provision of mental health services." In: Manpower for Mental Health. F. Arnhoff, E. Rubinstein and J. Speisman, Eds. Chicago: Aldine Publishing Company, 1969.

92. U.S. Government Printing Office. A report in Mental Health Digest, U.S. Government Printing Office, 1969. p. 50

93. Ellis, Havelock. Studies in the Psychology of Sex. New York: Random House. Volume I, Part I, 1905.

94. Kinsey, Alfred; Pomeroy, Wardell; and Martin, Clyde. Sexual Behavior in the Human Male. Philadelphia: W.B. Saunders Company, 1948.

95. Kinsey, Alfred, and Paul Gebhard. Sexual Behavior in the Human Female. Philadelphia: W.B. Saunders Company, 1953.

96. Masters, William, and Johnson, Virginia. Human Sexual Response. Boston: Little, Brown and Company, 1966.

97. Mathis, James. "The emotional impact of surgical sterilization of the female." Washington, D.C.: Mental Health Digest, 2, 8, August 1969. (Condensed from the Journal of the Oklahoma State Medical Association, 62, 4, 1969.

98. Eichner, Edward. "The premenstrual tension syndrome—fact or fancy?" In: Psychosomatic Obstetrics, Gynecology and Endocrinology, William S. Kroger, Ed. Springfield, Illinois: Charles C Thomas, 1962. p. 319

99. Pollock, O. The Criminology of Women. Philadelphia: University of Pennsylvania Press, 1950.

100. Paige, Karen. "Women learn to sing the menstrual blues." Psychology Today, September, 1973.

101. Chodoff, Paul. "Psychological response to concentration camp survival." Psychological Aspects of Stress, Harry S. Abram, Ed. Springfield, Illinois: Charles C Thomas, 1970. p. 48

102. Dunbar, Flanders. Mind and Body: Psychosomatic Medicine. New York: Random House, 1955. p. 264

103. Ellis, Havelock. Studies in the Psychology of Sex. New York: Random House. Volume I, Part I, 1905. p. 14

104. Freeman, Lucy. What Do Women Want? New York: Human Sciences Press, 1978.

105. Knight, R.P., and Wright, T. Sexual Symbolism: A History of Phallic Worship. New York: The Julian Press, 1957.

106. Johnson, Warren. Human Sexual Behavior and Sex Education: Perspectives and Problems. Philadelphia: Lea and Febiger, 1968.

107. Beach, Frank. "Evolutionary aspects of psychoendocrinology." In: Behavior and Evolution, A. Roe and G. Simpson, Eds. New Haven: Yale University Press, 1958.

108. Masters, William, and Johnson, Virginia. In: "A Conversation with Masters and Johnson," by Mary Harrington Hall. Psychology Today, 1969. pp. 50-58

109. Masters, William, and Johnson, Virginia. Human Sexual Response. Boston: Little, Brown and Company, 1966. pp. 192-193

110. Masters, William, and Johnson, Virginia. "View sex comfortably, doctors told." The Miami Herald (and United Press International), 1972.

111. Landers, Ann. "Wife troubled by impotency." San Diego: The Evening Tribune, 1975.

112. Liepmann, William. Reported in: Feminine Psychology, by Karen Horney. New York: W.W. Norton and Company, Inc., 1967.

113. Masters, William, and Johnson, Virginia. In: "A conversation with Masters & Johnson," by Mary Harrington Hall. Psychology Today, 1969. pp. 50-58

114. Fenichel, Otto. The Psychoanalytic Theory of Neuroses. New York: W.W. Norton and Company, 1945.

115. Brown, Frank A. "The rhythmic nature of animals and plants." Scientific American, 47, 1959.

116. Greenwald, Harold, Direct Decision Therapy. San Diego: EdITS, 1973.

117. Seligman, Martin. "Fall into helplessness." Psychology Today. June, 1973.

118. Rochlin, Gregory. Griefs and Discontents; The Forces of Change. Boston: Little, Brown and Company, 1965.

119. Rochlin, Gregory. Man's Aggression; The Defense of Self. Boston: Gambit, 1973.

120. Lerner, Max. Values in Education. Bloomington, Indiana: The Phi Delta Kappa Educational Foundation, 1976. p. 20

121. Wheelis, Allen. "How People Change." New York: *Commentary,* May 1969.

INDEX

D

E

F

G

H

I

N

O

DR. FAUST, nationally recognized educator and psychologist, describes the edge of a breakthrough destined to propel education into a new age. Its impact reaches far beyond schools, destined to forge a new society. "What happens in our schools today," he reminds us, "becomes tomorrow's world."

Dr. Faust paints an intriguing landscape that will provoke your imagination and spark your determination to become a part of the imminent, long-overdue breakthrough in education.

Dr. Faust offers convincing evidence that most learning problems will become relics of a forgotten era when teachers introduce consistent, sure ways for themselves and students to maintain a full sense of self-esteem. "Whatever else the learning process is, its core is self-esteem, and the heart of self-esteem can be found in how we evaluate students." After exposing the cruel effects wrought by current evaluation methods, he supplies a practical, down-to-earth approach that nurtures self-esteem, insuring the learner against failure.

"No force — political, economic, militaristic or religious — holds the potential for shaping a healthy, vibrant society, mostly free of learning deficiencies, crime, self-destruction, personal unhappiness, racism, bigotry, civil strife and the slaughter of world wars, than do the schools. Aside from the home, it is the schools which are, by far, the major energy in the world.

"It's impossible to get inside each home, or a significant number of them, to help parents behave with their youngsters in ways that prevent learning and discipline problems. Therefore it remains for teachers to provide a climate which will get the job done. This effort must be based on the realization that yesterday's childhood is today's society—one that has in it far more destructive influences than can be tolerated much longer.

"What happens between teachers and students is of critical importance to human and social welfare. It is here, only here, that a significant breakthrough can be made in the kind of world we have; whether in fact we will not only survive but survive well."

THOMAS PAINE PRESS

6674 Danville Avenue
San Diego, California 92120

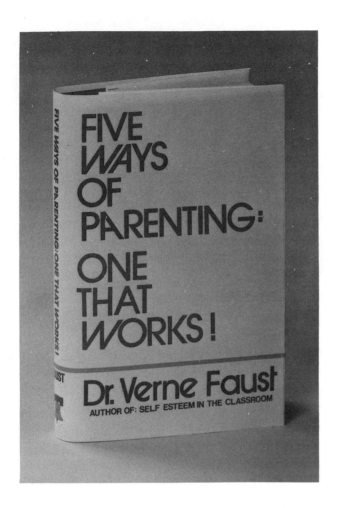

"Today's children are tomorrow's future." Concerned for that future and a more rewarding, satisfying present, Dr. Faust, educator and clinical psychologist, licensed by the California Board of Medical Examiners, reveals a new dimension to parenting long overdue. His extensive work with families in clinical and educational settings has revealed five ways of parenting, described here in vivid, unforgettable detail. These five categories, discovered through broad experience, encompass all parenting techniques used today.

Though parents combine several of the types, Dr. Faust has discovered that each parent depends on one more often than the others. Four of these methods have been found to be destructive and are innocently passed from one generation to the next. They lead to learning problems, behavior disorders, bed-wetting, allergies, delinquency and chronic illness. In familiarizing yourself with the four destructive methods, you speed up understanding of the fifth type.

Integrating research with experience, Dr. Faust introduces a down-to-earth way of parenting — a fifth dimension — that offers you and your offspring a new kind of relationship, enhancing self-esteem. It provides opportunities for a more satisfying, productive life and physical well-being. The "fifth dimension" is simple, yet will intrigue and provoke you. In one way or another, after you read *Five Ways of Parenting,* you will never be the same again.

Dr. Faust discusses in detail an alternative to the first four kinds of parents, ONE THAT WORKS! In clearly stated terms he leads you into impact-centered methods of parenting.

Dr. Faust explains what the IMPACT PARENT believes about human beings and what they must have in order to function effectively in work, play, learning and love! He describes practical methods of turning theory into practice.

Five Ways of Parenting: One That Works is a concrete, daily guide to better relationships with children and teenagers, one that pays off for everyone. The remarkable result of impact parenting is that youngsters become the sort of healthy, self-responsible persons that society hopes for but fails to achieve with product-centered spanking methods.

Not only is learning potential released through impact parenting but greater, more effective self-discipline is achieved, one that works constructively for society."

THOMAS PAINE PRESS

6674 Danville Avenue
San Diego, California 92120